S0-BII-119

To help mend the bodies, minds and souls of the children of Afghanistan, I am donating all proceeds from the sale of this book to International Orphan Care. This organization is dedicated to caring for and educating the Afghan children who have suffered through the wars which have rocked their country over the last 2 decades.

Thank you for joining me.

Pres Darby

# Tears of the Oppressed

*An American Doctor In Afghanistan*

by Preston Darby, M.D.

1400 Doral Ct.
San Angelo, TX 76904

Coypright 2002
All Rights Reserved
ISBN 0-9676497-1-4
Second Edition

Printed by
Company Printing
San Angelo, Texas
888-825-5175

## *DEDICATION*

The Berlin wall is down, the Cold War is over, the Soviet Bear has retreated. One of the victims it ravaged——Afghanistan——was left embroiled in civil chaos, the result of inter-tribal wars and U.S. inattention. But for one shining hour, soon forgotten, the Afghan mujahideen, "Soldiers of God," stood united against a common enemy. These ragged, ill-equipped, legendary fighters defeated the previously unstoppable Soviet superpower and regained their homeland. For a time I shared their struggles, their triumphs, and their tragedies.

This story is respectfully dedicated to those Afghan Soldiers of God who saved my life, saved their country, and changed the world.

# ACKNOWLEDGEMENTS

The preparation of this book was largely a solo effort and I take full responsibility for errors in style and substance; however, the task could not have been completed without the invaluable help of several people.

Steve Jones patiently provided frequently needed repairs and consolation during my first experience with a computer. The word processor remains an enigma.

The chapters on Afghan history and the Soviet invasion could not have been written without the detailed knowledge and assistance of my friends, Gulpadcha Mohabbat ("Pasha"), who survived the invasion and its aftermath, and Hasan Nouri, who has done more for his Afghan countrymen than anyone I know.

Jay Farrington, through his lectures and friendship, fanned a feeble spark to convince me that this project was feasible, then introduced me to Sara Clark. This kind and erudite lady, in spite of great personal travail, provided the framework and criticism which transformed a dog-eared, hastily scribbled journal into a readable account.

Several editors, most notably Ken Hodgson, aided in the preparation of the initial manuscript and its publication.

Mary and Ken Casper patiently directed and encouraged my rewriting of the initial text into its present form and publication.

Thank you all!

Let me tell you a story of how boyhood dreams come true, events in a far-off land affect our whole world, and how just a couple of months in a lifetime can mold one's future in strange ways. And too, how God sometimes enters our lives with thunder and lightning, but also quietly, subtly, as doors that open and close.

# PREFACE

*"Oh God, from the venom of the cobra, the teeth of the tiger, and the vengeance of the Afghan, deliver us.*

—Old Hindu saying

The Soviets should have known better. But they ignored the Afghan experience of invaders who had failed and the reasons for their disastrous defeats.

Geography and the ethnic groups of Afghanistan create a decentralized tribal society. The eastern and northern regions are composed of high mountains surrounding narrow rocky valleys; the southern and western areas are forbidding deserts. Over ninety per cent of the population lives in rural rugged terrain with a harsh climate. The people have little faith in their central government. Their tribal society is ruled by *Khans*, or local commanders *(Malik)*. Disputes are settled by *jirgahs*, or discussions, with the rule of *Khans* being almost absolute.

Each Afghan reflects his heritage. He is fiercely independent, with allegiance only to his tribe and Allah and follows a personal code of honor, revenge and hospitality. For an Afghan, failure to seek revenge is regarded as loss of honor and honor is the core of each Afghan's thinking. These traits, combined with the harsh environment provided a fertile field for the rapid and early growth of the *mujahideen* resistance to the Soviet invasion. Each guerrilla could be supplied from nearby sources since the Afghan code of hospitality ensured the local populace would support any resistance group, even if the group was not from its area. In accordance with the Muslim tradition, at least ten per cent of all produce and two-and-a-half per cent of yearly earnings were set aside by each Afghan family as its share to support the *mujahideen*. Their mastery of weapons, ability to survive in rugged terrain, and their code make them a formidable foe.

The extensive Soviet bombing and brutal scorched earth policy, however, soon reduced the ability of the people to support themselves, much less the resistance movement. In rural areas medical care, primitive at best, was rendered almost non-existent. Of approximately 1,200 physicians practicing in Afghanistan before the invasion, only 200 were left after the Soviet purge. In the cities intellectuals were imprisoned, tortured, and executed. Indiscriminate bombing of the countryside and devastation by ground forces drove five to six million people out of the country into Pakistan or Iran. Well over a million Afghans out of the pre-war population of 16 million were killed outright. Many of those remaining inside Afghanistan left their homes and moved into the mountains to eke out a primitive existence for their family. They supported the *mujahideen* to the best of their abilities and raised opium poppies as a "money crop."

Resistance parties had been formed prior to the Soviet invasion. By late 1979 six groups had been established with their headquarters in Pakistan. As might be expected from the fiercely independent Afghan nature, frequent bickering and disagreement between the party leaders occurred, particularly between fundamentalist members of the Muslim brotherhood and more moderate theologians. Leaders in Iran made a serious effort to impose their influence on some of the groups but were largely unsuccessful, and as time passed, pro-western countries in the region extended their support to the resistance movement.

The Soviets made another miscalculation. With their power and influence, as well as their serious infiltration into the management of Afghan armed forces, they apparently believed the Afghan communists would fight along with the Soviet troops as ferociously as their heritage dictated. Again, the invaders should have remembered history. In 1882, an Englishman, Edward Hensman, praised the individual Afghan fighting man but noted, "Once he is asked to abandon his identity and merely become a unit in a battalion, he loses all self-confidence and is likely to think more of getting away than stubbornly holding his ground as he would have done with his own friends led by his own chief." (quoted in David Isby, *War in A Distant Country*, 1988). The Afghan communist army for the most part fought poorly, since most of the younger Afghans joined only to acquire a weapon, then deserted to join one of the resistance groups.

Unable to defeat the individual, locally led guerrilla forces, the Soviets changed their tactics to massive ground sweeps supported by helicopters and instituted a brutal scorched-earth policy. Their conventional tactics worked well in open terrain but failed miserably in the unforgiving narrow valleys.

Land was laid waste so effectively that the occupants were compelled to abandon their homes and farms for refuge in the high mountains or surrounding countries, ending local support for the resistance troops.

Casualties were heavy among the invading troops, especially against the military genius of Ahmad Shah Massoud, the charismatic resistance leader in the Panjshir Valley. Massoud's constant successes ultimately resulted in a negotiated truce lasting from January 1983 until the spring of 1984.

Another decisive turning point in the war occurred in April 1984 when the seventh Soviet assault on the Panjshir Valley failed. Massoud's successes sent a message of hope to the other resistance groups, and the fight continued. Early Soviet war plans called for the subjugation of Afghanistan within six months. After five years Soviet forces were hopelessly bogged down.

The Soviets tried everything short of nuclear weapons. From the first days of the war, lethal chemical warfare agents were used, unspeakable atrocities were inflicted on the local population, and the land was laid waste; but the Afghans fought on.

Terror was used as a deliberate weapon. "Butterfly" anti-personnel mines were sown into the fields indiscriminately to kill and maim children; water supplies were poisoned; farm animals were killed; villagers were captured, tortured and executed. Still the mujahideen would not yield. Western countries, including the United States, began to realize that the spirit and effectiveness of the Afghan resistance provided an excellent opportunity to make the Soviets "bleed a little." Weapons and supplies poured through various covert routes to the Afghan forces. Often such equipment was shoddy, out of date, and very little use, but the Afghans adapted it to their needs and continued not only to survive, but to inflict severe damage on the technologically superior invaders.

Medical help for the freedom fighters was initially provided by the few remaining native physicians and French volunteers of "Doctors Without Borders," which furnished physicians and nurses for the embattled country. In spite of the heroic efforts of this excellent organization, the maxim prevailed: "To be wounded in Afghanistan is to die in Afghanistan." Many European countries supplied medical help to the growing refugee population in Pakistan, and American organizations joined this effort.

An unbelievably courageous Afghan physician, Dr. Abdullah Osman, escaped from Afghanistan with his family but later re-entered the country to document the appalling conditions and atrocities. Through a mutual friend and staunch supporter of the Afghan resistance, Mr. Hasan Nouri, Dr. Osman's report reached the attention of Dr. Robert Simon, an American physician of Lebanese origin, who was training Emergency Room physicians at UCLA. Dr.

Simon visited Peshawar, Pakistan, in 1984, and entered Kunar Province in Afghanistan to observe first-hand the desperate need for medical personnel. Upon his return, Hasan Nouri, Dr. Simon, and their associates founded the International Medical Corps to send American physicians and nurses to Afghanistan. Reports such as those of Dr. Simon and Dr. Osman, plus articles by European journalists, publicized the genocide being inflicted by the Soviet invaders. As a result, in late 1984, the Soviet Ambassador to Pakistan stated publicly in Islamabad: "I warn you, and through you, all your...colleagues about trying to penetrate Afghanistan with so-called *mujahideen*. From now on, the bandits and the so-called journalists, the French, the Americans, or the British and others that accompany them will be killed and our units in Afghanistan will help the Afghan forces do it."

Soon the price in Afghanistan for an American journalist alive or dead was $12,000; for an American doctor, $10,000.

# CHAPTER 1

In late 1984 I was planning to work for the Episcopal Church in the Dominican Republic when I chanced on an article in a medical newspaper about Doctor Bob Simon who was recruiting volunteer physicians and nurses for Afghanistan. Impulsively I sent a letter to Doctor Simon offering my services. To my surprise, he promptly accepted. Travel would be at my own expense, he said, and, in the understatement of the century, advised there would be "an element of danger."

Since I was in solo practice and had never left the office for more than four or five consecutive days, I felt that one month's absence would be the maximum and so informed Bob. By mid-November all necessary arrangements had been made, and I was scheduled to leave in January, 1985. Time was short; therefore I stepped up my early morning jogging and weight training, for at age fifty-four I knew that good physical condition would be essential. In retrospect I can say it was probably life-saving.

I searched the library and old National Geographic magazines for information about Afghanistan, but found very little. It was a country of deserts in the western part, with a towering, forbidding mountain barrier to the east. Even the name suggested remoteness, inaccessibility and danger.

Because my information was so limited, particularly concerning progress in the war against the Soviets, I called my younger brother, Ted, recently retired from the CIA, to see what information he could provide from his source.

Ted's succinct reply: "Don't go!"

Later in December I received word from Bob Simon that a January trip was too hazardous. Intense warfare was reported along the Afghan border and supply routes. There also was credible evidence that the Soviets were using chemical agents in the areas we would have to cross. The trip was postponed until June.

Pam and I had been married less than three years, and our second child was due in mid-April. She would need another Cesarean section. Originally we had agreed I would go in January since I would be home before the baby came. Understandably, Pam didn't want me to be away when she was busy with two small children, as she would be in the summer. The trip was off.

Unexpectedly, in late January, 1985, I was contacted by Dr. Simon and asked if I could be ready to go to Afghanistan by early March. Pam agreed, as long as I would be home before our child was due. Arrangements were made to cover my practice while I was away, and I began exercising with even more vigor. A tourist visa to Pakistan was obtained by claiming I was going there to work in the mushrooming refugee camps along the border with Afghanistan. I bought an $1,800 round trip ticket to Peshawar, Pakistan, and as instructed, made no mention of any interest beyond providing some medical care to the unfortunate refugees surrounding that city.

Next, an ominous letter arrived from Dr. Simon' office advising me to dye my hair black, grow a beard, dye it black, and cover my blue eyes with brown contact lenses. I would be smuggled across the border, hoping to avoid the Soviets, the KGB and our State Department which objected vigorously to any Americans entering Afghanistan. A French physician working in that country had recently been captured by the Communists, sentenced to death, paraded through Kabul, the capital city, and then released to his government after the publicity value of such an incident had been achieved. The US State Department certainly did not want any such embarrassment.

To counter the grim news of the letter from the International Medical Corps, I was told that a documentary film would be made of my work in Afghanistan. Television anchorman, Stan Atkinson and his cameraman from station KRBC in Sacramento would meet me in Pakistan and discuss the details. Stan had reported recent events in the warring nations of Africa, was a world traveler, and had visited Afghanistan some years earlier. He would make me a movie star of me—or so I was told.

By the afternoon of March 7, my hair was cut very short and dyed; I had a week's start on my beard, and I was fitted with brown contact lenses. After purchasing jeans, T-shirts, underwear and hiking boots, I crammed all these into my backpack with old jogging shoes, a jacket, two cameras with lots of film, and a notebook. I was ready.

Now my plans were definite. Since I was leaving San Angelo the next day, it was time to inform my older children, John and Cathy. John lived in Dallas and managed a restaurant; Cathy was married and teaching at an elementary school in Lubbock. I was very concerned about their reaction to their middle-aged Dad going off on such a risky venture, but both children were supportive and loving as always.

"If this is something you want to do, go for it. But be careful, and come back in one piece."

For the past week I had awakened almost every night sweating from nightmares of attacks by Soviet gun ships, or being trapped in a cave digging frantically to escape. One night I dreamed in vivid color of being seated at a large banquet table with many turbaned Afghans. Far down the table to my left, a man reached for a piece of food with an enormous hand. His face below the black turban was distorted by the typical facial appearance of advanced acromegaly, a pituitary gland disorder that renders a person gigantic with coarse Neanderthal-like features. In the dream I turned to the person on my immediate right and said, "That man over there has acromegaly."

He replied, "Yes, he does. He does."

I awoke in a sweat. Pam roused for a moment, and I told her of the strange dream. Then I shot up in bed and realized it hadn't *all* been a dream. I <u>was</u> going half way across the world leaving behind a pregnant wife and small son. Still somewhat confused, I went to the bathroom mirror. I truly had dyed my hair and whiskers, and did look, as Pam had said jokingly, like a Yugoslavian child molester. For the rest of that night, I tossed and turned, trying to think of some excuse to call Bob Simon and tell him I couldn't go.

I must have dozed off, for I awoke again just before dawn with a terrible cold. I took a long hot shower, knowing it would probably be the last one for some time. The beard itched terribly and I felt awful. Pam and I had very little to say en route to the airport; each of us were lost in our own thoughts. We couldn't endure long good-byes. As I got out of the car she said simply, "I love you. You better come back to me."

Through the tears, I could only say, "No matter what happens I'll be back."

# CHAPTER 2

Entering the Pakistani International Airlines section at Kennedy Airport, I felt as if I had already left the US. No English was spoken except by the attendants, and I felt conspicuously out of place in my American clothes. We were advised that there would be no pork or alcohol available on the plane and the first leg of our journey would be to Paris or Frankfurt. Apparently the airline would decide which destination after the departure.

After a tediously boring delay, the long night flight to Germany began. I was seated next to an extremely large but very pleasant lady from Istanbul with a charming small daughter who took an immediate shine to me.

I enjoyed the movie, "Romancing the Stone," little realizing that I'd see it many times before the trip ended. The Pakistani in-flight meal was delicious, although I had no idea what I was eating. The coffee was strong enough to have raised Lazarus.

Unable to sleep, I spent the night holding the small child, thinking of home and trying to imagine things to come.

We arrived with the dawn at Frankfurt, refueled, and then flew on to Istanbul. I passed the time baby-sitting or dozing through the endless reruns of "Romancing the Stone."

Security was so lax in Frankfurt I could have smuggled a small howitzer on board, but not in Istanbul. If the Turkish guard who examined me as I left the plane had searched my person much longer, I would have felt that we had become engaged. Although I was in full view of the guard the entire time, I was again searched thoroughly before reboarding. But I was grateful for the security, particularly when I returned to the plane and found that my tickets, which I had dropped by my seat, were undisturbed.

We flew on to Syria and enjoyed a short respite in the Damascus terminal. Bags and bodies were again searched before returning to the plane. I did note that women were not searched, providing a great opportunity for female terrorists. But there was no way to ponder this disturbing thought while speeding on to Islamabad. There had not been a moment since leaving Frankfurt that some child wasn't screaming, and the johns were never empty except when changing occupants. From the number of children on board, I surmised there would always be a Pakistan.

At 4:00 a.m. local time, tired, sleepy and smelly, I arrived in Islamabad. Passport officials were no friendlier than in Istanbul as I was officially processed into Pakistan. Baggage retrieval was chaotic, with everyone pushing, pulling and shrieking an unintelligible language, but at least my luggage came through intact.

I spied two Americans in the crowd and introduced myself to the documentary film-maker, Stan Atkinson, and his cameraman, Emory Clay. Stan and Emory were staying in Islamabad a few days to film background interviews, before flying on to meet me in Peshawar.

Bidding them good-bye, I dragged my belongings through the mob and customs to the other end of the terminal, fending off persistent beggars and taxi drivers. After an hour or more fitfully dozing in line waiting to check in for the flight to Peshawar, my final destination, I was told it wouldn't book for at least four or more hours. I couldn't leave my bags even to go to the rest room, had nothing to read and was dead tired. Therefore I simply sat, stared and daydreamed of what might be facing me, and remembered all that I had left behind.

The loudspeakers rasped an unintelligible boarding call mentioning Peshawar, abruptly ending my reverie. I joined a group shuffling sleepily onto the tarmac and was hustled into a small, high-winged commuter plane of uncertain vintage. After mercifully brief incomprehensible instructions from a robed stewardess we roared through the dawn to Peshawar. The countryside reminded me of West Texas and northern Mexico with irrigated fields and adobe villages, but mostly dry, featureless plains.

Even though we landed shortly after daylight, the airport in Peshawar was packed. The constant shrieking of vendors blended with the din of crying children. This bedlam was punctuated by the roar of Russian-made MIGs leaving the adjacent Pakistani Air Force Base to patrol the Afghan border. After two days and nights en route I was tired and becoming more and more irritable as I pressed through the crowd looking for someone to meet me. I had only a name, "Nasir," to contact, and a phone number in Los Angeles if all our plans fell through.

Suddenly from behind me someone whispered, "I am Nasir."

I turned and the name I had traveled half way around the world to hear became a person. A handsome Afghan wearing a dark turban and pajama-like clothes stood just behind me. He was a head shorter than I, but insisted on carrying my backpack, camera bag and suitcase.

"Quickly, quickly, we must get to the safe house fast!" he said, "KGB men are everywhere."

Nasir, I, and two silent Afghans wedged ourselves into a toy-like Suzuki jeep holding my luggage in our laps. Nasir spoke to the driver, and we roared out of the parking lot ignoring shouts and gestures from the crowd.

It was immediately apparent that Afghans drive like they fight, without fear or regard for their safety or anyone else's. The small jeep tore through the traffic on the left side of the street and squealed around traffic circles. I closed my eyes when we rocketed through crowds of people, animals, trucks and thousands of Toyota sedans. The driver whipped down one-lane alleys forcing cursing pedestrians into the fetid ditches, which I soon realized were open sewers. We wound through a labyrinth past fierce looking bearded tribesmen who guarded the hideouts of high-ranking officials with Kalashnikov automatic rifles.

Our driver slid to a dusty stop in front of a two-story concrete building surrounded by an eight-foot wall, which enclosed a small yard and badminton court. This was to be my "safe house," where I would be isolated while in Peshawar. I was ushered into a tiny bedroom containing a couple of cots and was relieved to find we did have an indoor bathroom of sorts. There was a sink, a mirror and a faucet which sometime worked. Flies were everywhere. The toilet was an open hole in the floor, but did have a tank of water over it which would flush—when there was water. I learned later it emptied into an open ditch that drained through the yard. Although my nose was very congested from my cold, spicy odors from the kitchen and the musty smell of damp woolen prayer blankets overwhelmed me. The constant chatter of a strange language was punctuated with frequent slamming of the metal gate. Adding to the ear-splitting cacophony was the constant barking of large guard dogs outside our walls.

Dr. Simon had stressed that Afghans are known for their fierceness in battle as well as their hospitality, and I was soon to experience the latter. Shaking hands with everyone was a ritual, and many of the chieftains who came and went enveloped me in bear hugs. Not understanding a word that was first about the cheek kissing, and then decided, *Who cares? Nobody knows me here*, and kissed back.

The cook brought out platters of food, and I was introduced to *kabuli*, a delicious concoction of boiled rice containing strips of carrots, raisins, and small slivers of meat. By mid-morning I had become a tea lover. Hot tea was served in shallow glasses with enough sugar to fill the glass almost half way. Initially, the mixture was like drinking syrup, but as the glasses were refilled with the steaming liquid the sweetness was diluted, and each sip became tastier.

After meeting scores of people and sitting quietly, smiling and not understanding a word of the animated conversation, jet lag hit me and I took a two-hour nap, followed by a tepid shower.

Nasir and I left with our driver for another break-neck trip, this time to the bazaar—a scene seemingly ripped from an Arabian Nights movie. Crowded shops sold everything from pistachios to jewels. The aroma of curry, pepper, and spices floating over the booths was heaven-sent after the olfactory onslaught of the streets and gutters.

My disguise was soon completed by the purchase of a *kameez*, the loose fitting all-purpose garment with long sleeves which hangs outside the pants to the ankles. The pants were made with a waist size that would accommodate two or three people, and was cinched in with a drawstring. The whole outfit was wonderfully comfortable and cool. The hat *(pakul)* was a cylinder of wool rolled up and worn at a jaunty angle, with a flat top like a pie plate. In my new costume, I felt as though I blended better with the locals and attracted less interest.

Back at the safe house the Afghans were playing badminton with typical fierceness and noise. Although they repeatedly tried to coax me into the contest, I knew my clumsiness was no match for these experts.

Fortunately, a few of our visitors spoke some English. I was able to follow the gist of their conversations and took notes in my journal. By late evening I was exhausted but excited, still feeling a little jet lag, since the local time was approximately eleven hours in advance of Texas time. The evening was made much more pleasant by putting through a phone call to Pam. Everyone sat quietly and listened while I talked. We knew the phone was tapped, so our conversation was somewhat limited; but at least I learned she and everyone else at home were well.

Following the telephone call I met Colonel Osmani, formerly a colonel in the Afghan Tank Corps and an instructor at the Afghan War College before the Russians invaded. Osmani would play a large role in my adventures. Present also was Dr. Daoud Kabir, an anesthesiologist who had lost two fingers on his right hand in a mortar attack during a December trip inside Afghanistan. Since he still suffered from causalgia, a painful irritation of the nerves in his arm, we discussed a possible consultation for him in San Antonio with a hand surgeon. In contrast to the polite and accommodating Afghans I had met so far, Daoud tended to be somewhat overbearing and opinionated.

Just as I planned to go to bed, a most impressive visitor arrived. This leader was greeted with much respect, hugging, cheek kissing and general excitement.

Dr. Hashmet entered wearing a black turban, with a brocade vest and a tan corduroy coat over his *kameez*. He seemed the epitome of an Afghan intellectual. Highly educated and articulate, he spoke excellent English and talked at length about plans for my trip, then briefed me about the war and Russian attempts to change Afghan religious beliefs. He was distressed at recent bombing along the border and the loss of a vital ammunition factory and storage facility, apparently sabotaged by the KGB.

As usual, our evening meal was succulent, with mounds of spiced dark rice full of chicken, plus green peas and carrots cooked with chunks of meat, along with large bowls of thick, white yogurt. Dessert consisted of bananas, sweet oranges and green tea *(sheen choi)*. I drank glass after glass of the delicious sweet tea, and stuffed myself with *nan*, a toasted wheat bread similar to a flour tortilla.

The quality and quantity of food provided for each meal by Khalifa, our cook, was truly amazing. He toiled in a small room, the size of a clothes closet over a two-burner propane stove. With less than a half-dozen pots and pans plus one kettle he daily provided gallons of tea as well as three substantial meals for six to thirty hungry men. Each evening while residents of the house were playing badminton or swatting flies, Khalifa would walk several miles to the market for the next day's raw materials. He was treated with great respect and deference by all of the Afghans and me, for his services and continued good humor were essential to our welfare.

I had thought for days that "Khalifa" was his name, but later learned that it was a term of great respect, translated to me as meaning "Boss."

Cups were non-existent and our tea was usually served in shallow glasses. Sometimes we ate off of chipped porcelain plates; sometimes we heaped our portion on a tortilla-sized piece of nan. The latter method substantially reduced the number of dishes to be washed by the indefatigable Khalifa.

After the large meal and discussion I was exhausted and went to bed around 10:00 p.m., rolled up in my new *patoo* (prayer blanket) and dozed until dawn. I was awakened by the Muslim alarm clock—morning call from the nearby mosque.

At breakfast I attempted a conversation with Colonel Osmani. He spoke five languages but no English, so we struggled to converse using his fluent and my limited college German.

Later in the morning I was taken by a jeep to tour the "EMT" training facility. For the first but certainly not the last time I was touched and impressed by the dedicated young Afghan men who had walked out of their war-torn country to the school in Peshawar. In only six weeks they would master enough medical skills to provide basic care to the sick and wounded of their homeland. Classes were held in ragged tents, using rudimentary textbooks and anatomy mannequins donated by the International Medical Corps.

Next we visited a school for little girls, particularly impressive as the Afghan culture tended to leave most women uneducated. The headmaster of the school, Mr. Kasem, explained that with so many young men lost in the war, the future of Afghanistan would depend upon its women. Their classes were likewise held in tattered old tents.

I was fascinated by the girl's beauty, especially their luminescent dark eyes, and their ability to read the American alphabet and recite it perfectly. As a reward for their performance I gave them the dried fruit and candy I had brought along for my trip. Several girls were blue-eyed blondes, but I was unable to learn if these beauties were Nuristanis—allegedly descendants of Alexander the Great's Greek troops.

By afternoon I was weary and felt as if my face was frozen into perpetual smile after all the tours. We returned to the safe house, and I was able to nap for a couple of hours.

I awoke refreshed and soon had the pleasure of meeting Dr. Quadratullah Nasraty, who would become one of my closest friends. This very knowledgeable and handsome young surgeon spoke excellent English and had a wry sense of humor much like my own, so we spent the evening exchanging favorite jokes.

When the crowd diminished later that evening, I tried for an hour or more to help Colonel Osmani place a phone call to his wife in Paris but never could make connections. Nevertheless, he seemed to be grateful for my efforts, and I knew I had made another friend.

By Tuesday, March 12, five days had passed since my departure from home. Jet lag was diminishing, sleep at night was sustained, and I didn't have the feeling in early afternoon that someone had pulled my plug. My cold had disappeared, and I felt well.

After breakfast we visited the Union of Afghan *Mujahideen* Physicians' headquarters. I was very touched to learn they had voted me into their organization. My companions and I were discussing plans for our trip when a young American journalist arrived and proceeded to interview the group, mistaking me for an Afghan. I was very pleased my disguise was effective and will never forget the look on his face when he tried to speak to me in broken Pashto and I replied, "Howdy pardner!"

Shortly thereafter I made my first visit to a refugee camp on the outskirts of Peshawar. It was a depressing place of sagging tents, lean-tos and open latrines. Our clinic was held in one of the more patched and dilapidated shelters.

Each patient required a snap diagnosis obtained through an interpreter who had no knowledge of medical terms, followed by a *very* limited physical examination. For example, I could only take the pulse and blood pressure of the women and listen to their lungs through layers of clothing, closely monitored by a glowering, suspicious husband. I handed out lots of pills, mostly innocuous vitamins, which were no more effective than placebos. This hocus-pocus medicine would be my *modus operandi* inside Afghanistan. Such encounters may have been beneficial from the psychological and diplomatic perspectives, but they were certainly frustrating and unscientific for an American internist.

Late in the afternoon we made a mad dash to the Intercontinental Hotel to meet Stan Atkinson and plan the documentary. It was slated to begin with the plight of the refugees and the ghastly medical conditions in their camps. Unfortunately we couldn't locate Stan or Emory. I was sweaty and dirty after the long day's work and eager for a shower, but once again there was no water, hot or cold, at our house. Dr. Osman, the Afghan psychiatrist whom I'd met the previous day, graciously permitted me to take a quick shower at his hotel.

Eight of us then squeezed into the tiny Suzuki and caromed through town at breakneck speed to join an Afghan banquet. I wished the others in the car had had time to shower.

We were seated in the floor in a large rectangular room with Kalashnikov rifles hanging on the walls above us as the TV spoke of Soviet Premier Chernenkov's death. All evening my comments went back and forth through an interpreter, so it was very difficult to function as a diplomat; however, I must have succeeded to some extent because I received a beautiful Afghan rug from our host when we left.

The next morning we were up early and returned to the bazaar through choking dust and a mob scene of garishly painted buses, trucks and motorized rickshaws. I strutted through the crowd, practicing my Afghan swagger and stern expression, happily noting how the mob parted before us. Returning from the bazaar, we passed a picturesque, well-tended British cemetery shaded by large leafy trees, which provided stark contrast to the native graveyard containing only piles of rocks with small flags as markers.

We found Stan at the Intercontinental Hotel and returned to the refugee camp with him and Emory. I began seeing patients again while Emory filmed my efforts and the surroundings.

I examined two babies who had been carried by their young mothers the entire 200-kilometer walk from Kabul. Their group had been strafed repeatedly by Soviet jets, and over forty people had been killed during the trek. The children I treated rarely cried, even when being examined. I suppose they were exhausted. After what they had already been through, nothing could hold any greater horror. Thinking of these children and their parents in such squalid surroundings following their terrible ordeal kept me depressed while we prepared to return to the safe house. As we drove away from the refugee camp, I recalled a verse from Ecclesiastes, "I saw the tears of the oppressed, and I saw how there was no one to comfort them." How could I help so many?

Stan and Emory joined our group back at our headquarters for a lengthy discussion of our plans for the upcoming trip. We were scheduled to leave for the border in two days. One of the Afghan chieftains presented me with a Russian Kalashnikov automatic rifle to take on our journey. But I felt my reason for being there was to save lives, not take them, so I declined his generous offer. Fortunately I was able to do so without offending him. Diplomacy was becoming easier for me, though I was impatient to get on with my medical work inside Afghanistan. The next morning everybody had something to do, and I was left alone in my room, bored and homesick. I couldn't find anything to read and no one in the house spoke English, so I spent the day correlating my notes on Afghan history and events leading to the Soviet invasion.

# CHAPTER 3

A country roughly the size of Texas, Afghanistan shares its borders with the former Soviet Union to the north, Iran to the west, and Pakistan to the south and southeast. A small portion, "the Camel's Neck," touches China to the northeast. As would be expected from its precarious geopolitical location, Afghanistan has been invaded repeatedly—but never conquered.

Alexander the Great arrived in 330 A.D. but withdrew, unable to subdue the unyielding tribesmen. An Arab invasion in 663 A.D. also failed.

Ghengis Khan and his Mongol forces were unable to destroy the Afghans during their campaign across Asia in 1220 A.D.

In 1838 the British invaded, and their army was almost annihilated. Only one soldier, a physician, survived the disastrous retreat from Kabul in 1842. The fierceness of the Afghans so impressed the British that Rudyard Kipling later wrote:

*When you're wounded and left on Afghanistan's plains,*
*and the women come out to cut up what remains,*
*just roll to your rifle and blow out your brains,*
*and go to your Gawd like a soldier.*

After the disaster of 1842, the British mounted a punitive expedition in 1870 which was largely unsuccessful, but a treaty was signed between the Afghans and British in 1883. Part of this agreement divided the land of the Pashton tribesmen in eastern Afghanistan, resulting in the envelopment of these Afghans inside the new borders of what later came to be Pakistan.

In 1947, when India won its independence from Great Britain, and Muslim Pakistan was established, the Afghans reclaimed their territory in the northwest all the way to the Attak River. The division of the land of the Pashtons had nettled the Afghans through the years, and this irritation provided a political crack for foreign interests to exploit.

Many events in the history of Afghanistan are explained more by the nature of the Afghan people than by invaders and external influences. Afghans are proud to the point of arrogance and devoutly religious. Ninety-five percent of their population is Muslim; the tiny remainder are Hindus and Catholics. As well known for their hospitality as their fierceness in battle, Afghans love *jiirgahs*, or loud discussions, and sports. *Buzkashi*, a wild and violent form of polo, is still the traditional sport, somewhat modified over the centuries. In times past, the *buzkashi* "ball" was a live captive, dragged up and down the playing field by opposing horsemen. Fortunately the modern version uses a calf or goat carcass. Soccer, volleyball, field hockey, and badminton entertain the less violent.

With very little industry except in the cities of Kabul and Kandahar, sites of the famous rug weavers and Astrakan furs, agriculture and sheep raising occupied most of the populace. The life style was simple. Generally comfortable and content, people concerned themselves very little with the machinations and intrigues of the central Afghan government.

In 1950, leaders in Kabul invited technical advisors including geologists and engineers from the United States to explore Afghanistan's natural resources. Unfortunately, the American government did not respond. The United Nations, however, did send specialists who discovered large deposits of gas and oil, particularly in the northern part of the country adjacent to the Soviet Union.

The Soviets promptly sent a letter of protest to the Afghan government claiming these exploring teams were CIA employees who were busily mapping the areas for military purposes. They insisted that the explorations cease and offered to send their own technicians. To avoid conflict, Mohammed Zahir Shah, the Afghan King, asked the U.N. teams to leave. He also ignored the Russian offer of assistance.

By 1951, the Soviets had become concerned over the increasing influence of the United States in the Middle East, the Far East and Asia, and felt they were losing control in these areas. Realizing Afghanistan could be the hub for operations to counter the perceived American threat, the Soviets began serious efforts to establish ties with the government of Afghanistan with two main objectives:

First, get closer to the warm water ports of the Persian Gulf and Indian Ocean, since the southern border of Afghanistan is only 350 kilometers from the gulf.

Second, participate in or control the exploitation of Afghanistan's natural resources since they were now convinced (because of the U.N. exploration) of the rich mineral, gas, and oil reserves in the country, as well as some cloaked reports of substantial high-grade uranium deposits.

Exploiting the Afghans' disappointment with the United States' refusal to help, the Soviets offered to send 350 geologists and 35 economists at no cost to the Afghans to assist in research and advise the central government. Actually, their covert plan was to infiltrate the entire infrastructure. The Afghan government accepted the proposition without a second thought and on May 26, 1951, several Soviet groups entered Afghanistan.

They performed their tasks rapidly and well. Detailed topographic maps were drawn, natural resources mapped, government offices infiltrated. Secret reports furnished strategic information for Soviet political maneuvers. Not surprisingly, the results of this research were not shared with the Afghans; however, the Soviet government began immediate action to reinforce their political alliance with Afghanistan.

On December 15, 1955, Soviet leaders Bulganin and Krushchev paid an official state visit to Kabul. The two countries signed several military, educational, and economic agreements. Mr. Bulganin stressed his hopes for the establishment of sincere friendships between the nations and emphasized that the Soviets had no wish to be involved in the internal affairs of its neighbor. However, he cleverly appealed to the Afghans' nationalistic pride by supporting their claims to the land of the Pashtons. Opening this old wound, Bulganin stressed how much the Afghan people resembled inhabitants of that region.

Soon after the Soviet delegation returned to Moscow, the Afghans re-instituted their old demands that the territory of Pashtonistan be returned to Afghanistan. Tension increased with Pakistan and soon all diplomatic relations between the two countries were terminated. The vital flow of imports and exports between Pakistan and Afghanistan trickled to a standstill.

Relations between Afghanistan and the USSR improved rapidly, as did the buildup of military forces.

At the time, the Afghan military consisted of a few British-manufactured planes and five or six infantry divisions. Soon after Bulganin's visit, however, the number of infantry divisions increased, each well equipped with heavy and light weapons. The Afghan Air Force rapidly increased its personnel and aircraft. During 1957 and 1958, many young men were sent to Russia for military and civil training. They returned thoroughly indoctrinated with communist beliefs. Russian diplomats and KGB operators penetrated all levels of the Afghan government and major industries. The Afghan Secret Service finally lost control of its operations to the Soviet infiltrators.

For many years the Soviets had dreamed of seeing the Afghan government in this predicament. As trade with Pakistan withered, Afghans found themselves obliged to deal with the Soviets. The Soviets in turn monopolized every opportunity. Slowly they began to influence the political, economic and military affairs of the Afghan government, increasing the unrest between Pakistan and Afghanistan. In 1957, these countries put their armies on alert. Conflict was avoided only through the intervention of the United Nations.

The issue of Pashtonistan may seem minor, but it provided the Soviets with a win-win strategy. If the territory was ceded to Afghanistan, Pakistan (on good terms with the United States) would be reduced in size and strength. This change would also reduce the distance to the Indian Ocean and the Persian Gulf for the Soviets. If Pashtunistan were not separated from Pakistan, the tension would remain and the Soviets could readily exploit the deteriorating relations between the Afghans and the Pakistanis while infiltrating all levels of the Afghan government.

After 1960, the number of Afghan communists rapidly increased. The Soviets offered free medical care in Russia to the military staff and all ranking officials of the government. The KGB was able to infuse more and more of its programs and ideology into government policy and affect all levels of Afghan life. There remained one big problem – the resistance of the Afghan ruler, Mohammed Zahir Shah, to the growing Soviet influence. Initially, the Soviets worked to depose him, but this failed, due largely to the King's loyal supporters in the military.

Trying another approach, Soviet agents exploited the shabby relationship between the king and Mohammed Daoud, the king's cousin and coincidentally his brother-in-law. Communist Afghans persuaded Daoud to instigate a *coup d'état* because of the poor economic conditions. Alerted to the plan, the king began clandestine preparations. Unfortunately he didn't take it seriously enough and left for a short trip to England. On July 17, 1973, while the king was in London for medical reasons, the *coup d'état* occurred.

Mohammed Daoud became President, promptly appointing Afghan communists to important posts in the Ministry of Defense. While the Soviets were not happy about a member of the royal family as leader, they provided prompt diplomatic recognition, sent him congratulations and invited him to

Russia. Even though he suspected that the Soviets were already plotting against him, President Daoud arrived in Moscow and was warmly welcomed by Leonid Brezhnev.

In the discussions that followed, Brezhnev asked Daoud why he continued to employ advisers from the imperialistic countries. Daoud responded that when he felt he could safely replace those advisors with his own people, he would send them all back—without exceptions.

Although Brezhnev seemed to be satisfied with this answer, he disagreed with many of Daoud's policies. After the visit, President Daoud became convinced the Soviets were working against him. He removed the communists in his personal staff but could not eliminate them from every level of government.

Next, in order to reduce the ties with the U.S.S.R., he paid state visits to Iran, Saudi Arabia, Libya, Egypt, Pakistan and Germany. In each country he requested financial and economic support. All of the Muslim countries and Germany pledged their help.

One of Daoud's cabinet members present during talks with the Shah of Iran and President Anwar Sadat of Egypt was Mr. Jal-la-lar, a Soviet spy. He promptly transmitted the contents of all discussions to the KGB. The Soviets were outraged. With the help of Afghan communists they began plans for another *coup.*

On April 27, 1978 the *coup* took place. Daoud and his family were assassinated, members of his cabinet were killed and others imprisoned. Mr. Noor Mohammed Taraki became President, and the communists took over the government. Shortly thereafter they ordered a massive execution of intellectuals, scientists, doctors, a great majority of the royal family and many religious leaders. Curfews were imposed, homes of the rich were looted, and *de facto* martial law was imposed.

When Taraki felt the situation was under control, he decided to show his loyalty and friendship to the Soviets by visiting Moscow accompanied by some of his cabinet members. Brezhnev congratulated Taraki, and gave him a warm reception as well as a Soviet hero's medal. In subsequent discussions, military and economic agreements were established. While relations in Moscow between the leaders were improving, back in Afghanistan the situation was steadily deteriorating.

The savage purges and tyrannical controls imposed by the communists inflamed the Afghan people. Those who could leave took refuge in the neighboring countries of Iran and Pakistan, while resistance groups formed in the cities and countryside. As the communists imposed increasingly draconian controls, the resistance groups became larger and stronger.

A battle for power within the communist leadership compounded the unrest. As a result, the government became increasingly unstable. Taraki's First Deputy, Babrak Karmal, was sent to Czechoslovakia as ambassador. Three months later, Afghan Radio announced that Karmal was a traitor and had plotted to overthrow the government. Many of Karmal's friends were jailed, others were executed and Karmal fled to Russia.

The power struggle continued. Hafizullah Amin, a war lord with dictatorial ambitions, replaced Karmal as First Deputy and was also assigned to the Ministry of Foreign Affairs and Defense. Without delay he ordered the execution of large numbers of anti-communists.

In late 1978 Taraki attended a conference of non-aligned countries in Havana. En route home he stopped in Moscow for a meeting with Brezhnev and Karmal. Brezhnev told the Afghans in no uncertain terms they were conducting the affairs of their nation in a childlike and incompetent manner, creating an embarrassment to the communist cause. He also said their government and the Afghan Communist Party were losing stability.

Brezhnev "suggested" Taraki and Babrak Karmal settle their differences and insisted Taraki get rid of Amin since Amin was suspected of having connections with the American CIA.

Traveling with Taraki was a friend of Amin, Major Taroon. As soon as Taraki and Taroon landed in Kabul, they met with Amin, who immediately sensed a change in Taraki's attitude toward him. Privately, Taroon warned Amin to be very careful and told him of the conversations with Brezhnev. Amin agreed to take precautions.

While Amin and Taraki were at the palace discussing the recent trip, the Russian Ambassador, Puzanov, phoned Taraki. When Amin was asked to leave the room, he realized the plot against him had begun and returned to his office at the Ministry of Defense. An hour later, Taraki called Amin and requested he come to his palace right away. Amin refused. Finally, Taraki and Puzanov, having decided to assassinate Amin, sent Taroon over in an attempt to persuade Amin to come to an important meeting.

Amin concealed a pistol in his clothing and went to the palace with an armed escort and Taroon as bodyguard.

As soon as Amin entered Taraki's office, the shooting began. In the melee the major and six others were killed. Amin was wounded in the shoulder but managed to escape to the Ministry of Defense. He placed his commanders on immediate alert and decreed they obey only his direct orders, ignoring all others. He then had them arrest Taraki.

When they learned of this action, the Afghan ministers of the interior, defense and communications, as well as the chief of the secret service left immediately for the sanctuary of the Russian and Czech embassies. From there they fled to Moscow. Amin promptly jailed the families of these men. Taraki was strangled in his cell. A few days later, Radio Kabul announced he'd died of "bad health." Puzanov instructed everyone concerned to classify as "Top Secret" all events in the presidential palace. Amin became president, blamed Taraki and his friends for past problems and promised to correct the situation.

Although the Soviets were disturbed by recent events, they sent a letter of congratulations to Amin. Amin pretended to be on good terms with the Soviets but ordered Ambassador Puzanov to leave Afghanistan. Next, he named his son-in-law, Assadullah Amin, as chief of the secret service. Assadullah promptly severed all communications between his organization and the Soviets. Two months after his appointment, Assadullah was wounded in an assassination attempt by a KGB agent. To convince the Soviets the two countries were on good terms, Amin sent Assadullah to Russia for treatment. In reality, relations between the two countries were rapidly worsening. On his return to Moscow, Puzanov gave a full report to Brezhnev of the recent happenings in Afghanistan, emphasizing that Amin was not a well disciplined or obedient Communist.

For the Soviets, invasion was the only solution. Earlier plans were implemented, and the previously unstoppable Soviet juggernaut began to roll.

General Pavlovsky, second Defense Minister, who had been in charge of the 1968 Soviet invasion of Czechoslovakia, General Paputin, First Deputy Minister of the Interior, General Pakrishkin, Chief of Staff of the Air Force, and General Mazarov, Chief of Staff of the Infantry began preparations for the invasion. As his first step, General Pavlovsky arranged a meeting with some of the Afghan refugees in the Soviet Union since they were very much opposed to Amin. With the help of the Afghan ministers who had recently arrived in Moscow, Pavlovsky also gathered and verified information concerning strategic sites in Afghanistan. He then met with his staff, developed the final invasion plan and presented all the data to Brezhnev. After reviewing the plan in detail, Brezhnev signed the necessary orders.

On November 28, 1979, General Paputin arranged a meeting with President Amin. At the same time, General Field Marshal Sergei Leanidovich and his forces began crossing the Amoo-Darya into Afghanistan.

Fifteen hundred soldiers accompanied by heavy artillery, trucks, and fuel tankers were airlifted to Bagram Airfield, fifty kilometers north of Kabul. Twelve hundred soldiers were flown to the airports of Shindand and Kandahar. Soviet troops were simultaneously massed in other strategic positions.

During his supposedly friendly meeting with Amin, General Paputin convinced the President his country should begin preparations to defend itself against the growing American influence. In reality, the Soviets feared the increasing infiltration of the communist Afghan army by members of the resistance movement. Paputin requested the transfer of control of all air bases and control towers to Soviet military advisers. He also proposed assignment of his agents to positions in the Afghan Secret Service and asked if all Soviet advisers and soldiers could wear Afghan Army combat uniforms. Next, he suggested a Soviet medical staff supervise food preparation for the army and for all the Afghan ministries.

General Paputin then warned Amin that according to Soviet recent information, the United States and Pakistan were planning to attack Afghanistan. He offered to put more fully equipped soldiers at Amin's disposal since the anti-Amin resistance was getting stronger every day. He strongly recommended that President Amin move to Darollaman Palace, situated on a hilltop eight kilometers west of Kabul and give orders for his soldiers to dig trenches and position tanks around Kabul.

Amin listened very carefully and accepted all the proposals except reinforcements. The Soviets had already stationed thousands of military advisers and soldiers at the various air bases in Afghanistan. To Amin, these numbers seemed quite sufficient to assure security.

After moving to the palace, Amin ordered his army to carry out Paputin's requests. The Soviet general returned to Moscow not completely satisfied with the developments but continued to make plans for the invasion.

Thirty-thousand soldiers were placed on alert at the mobilization center of Termez, just across the border from Afghanistan. On December 25, 1979, the Soviet government dropped leaflets all over the USSR saying in effect: The

Americans have invaded Afghanistan. Afghanistan is our neighbor; therefore, we are obliged to protect them.

On December 27, a Soviet doctor added sedatives to food prepared for Amin and his Imperial Guard at Darollaman Palace. The same day, an "air bridge" composed of about 150 AN-20 cargo planes delivered arms and personnel to the airports of Kabul and Bagram. At 1:00 p.m., the Soviet Minister of Communications, Nickolay Talyzin, paid a "friendly" visit to Darollaman Palace in order to dupe Amin. During the visit, Afghan tanks that had been parked around the Palace were moved to another location (Rish Khor) by order of the Soviet military advisers. Apparently, Amin was drugged or too busy with the visit to notice this move.

At 2:30 p.m., a flight of AN-22 transports delivered 2,000 soldiers to the airport in Kabul while 2,000 more landed at Bagram. After the planes were positioned on the field, the doors opened and soldiers filed out with perfect precision. A Soviet "advisor" was waiting who immediately directed the battalion to military and civil installations.

First, they disconnected all contact with the central station of communication. Afghan civilians and military personnel were forced from the buildings. Contact with the outside world was cut off.

Next, soldiers were dispersed to strategic points on the airports. By 5:00 p.m. they had complete control of security around the field, and another "air bridge" of over 150 transport planes brought in heavy and light artillery, tanks and more soldiers.

A large party in honor of the new Soviet Ambassador to Afghanistan was given at the Intercontinental Hotel with many high-ranking Afghan army officers in attendance. At 8:00 p.m., with Amin and his bodyguards still drugged and the party in full swing, military operations began at the Kabul airport, seven kilometers north of the city.

A bomb placed by the KGB destroyed the communications building, effectively severing all contact with the Afghan president, his ambassadors and the rest of the world. The explosion also signaled Soviet ground troops to begin moving into Kabul. On the outskirts of the city, their forces split. One group took over Radio Kabul, another surrounded the Ministry of Interior and a third group took over Pol-i-Charkhi prison, east of Kabul. Additional units moved toward the Afghan army division at Kargha, engaged the division stationed at Rish Khor and severed all strategic roads to Kabul. The city was isolated.

Led by General Paputin, a large contingent of Soviets surrounded Darollaman Palace and began shooting. After eight hours of fierce fighting, Paputin's troops reached the palace grounds and the firing ceased. Paputin got out of his truck and marched toward the entrance. One of Amin's bodyguards fired, wounding Paputkin in the right shoulder. Paputkin's force retaliated with a fusillade of shots killing Amin's defeuders. When Amin realized the situation, he fled his office but was killed by one of Paputkin's soldiers before he could escape. Paputkin was disturbed when he learned of Amin's death and agonized that he had somehow failed to accomplish his mission. On December 28, 1979, in circumstances still unexplained, General Paputkin was executed.

With the death of Amin, his government collapsed. Some of his ministers were killed, a few were taken prisoner, and others escaped to refugee camps. At 9:15 p.m. on December 28, 1979, the Soviets broadcast a pre-recorded speech from Babrak Karmal, who was in Russia at the time. The message was actually sent from a transmitter in Tashkent but used a frequency close to that of Radio Kabul. Karmal, leader of a Communist party named Parcham, declared he had taken over the Afghan government and was appealing for Soviet assistance. Meanwhile, Radio Kabul continued broadcasting normally, making no mention of the country's supposed change in leadership.

Not until early the morning of December 29 did the official Afghan broadcasting network announce the overthrow of President Amin by a "Revolutionary Tribunal" and his execution for "crimes against the people." Then Karmal's message was aired. During the next few violent days, close supporters of the Khalqi party not killed in the coup were thrown into Pul-i-Charkhi prison.

While Soviet troops were securing strategic positions in the capital, including the post office and the ammunition depots, the main Red Army thrust was coming from Termez, where General Sabolov had established field headquarters. At least 300 tanks and armored personnel carriers of the 360th Motorized Division, followed by a fleet of supply trucks, moved toward Kabul over the Soviet-constructed highway to the ancient strategically-placed city, Mazar-i-Sharif. Another armored column, the 201st Motorized Division, followed by the 16th Motorized Division, made its way toward Koundoz.

Here the column split; one unit moved toward Faizabad in Badakhshan Province, where guerrillas controlled much of the area. The other group roared south to the main Kabul highway. While long convoys of tankers provided much of the invasion forces' fuel requirements, Soviet engineers laid 30 kilometers of pipe along the Koundoz right-of-way to pump in petrol for the fast-moving troops.

At Koshk in western Afghanistan, the 66th Motorized Division, as well as elements of three other divisions, charged northward toward Herat, Shindand, and Farah before swinging east to Kandahar to join troops being airlifted to the American-built airport 12 kilometers outside the city.

The equivalent of two Soviet air divisions, more than four hundred aircraft, (mainly MIG-21, MIG-23, and SU-17 jet fighters, as well as MI-26 helicopter gunships) thundered back and forth over the main invasion area, providing an impenetrable umbrella. While the airlift constantly droned overhead, the first armored vehicles of the 306th began rumbling into the northern suburbs of Kabul. By dawn of the 28th of December, all important buildings and installations in the capital had been captured. Soviet troops also controlled strategic Salang Pass and the city of Pol-i-Khomri on the highway to Kabul from the Russian border. Soviet soldiers, Kalashnikov automatic rifles slung over their shoulders and supported by tanks, guarded intersections throughout Kabul and patrolled the streets. An 11:30 p.m. to 6:30 a.m. curfew was imposed. At the Kabul airport, a huge tent city packed with soldiers, supplies and vehicles had materialized along the frozen grass verges of the asphalt runways.

By the end of December, approximately 15,000 uniformed Soviet troops had established their quarters in and around the city of Kabul. Their command post was openly moved into the Soviet Embassy. After months of scheming and intrigue, the true agenda of the Soviets was revealed.

During the first few days of the occupation, they methodically consolidated their positions. With stunning rapidity, they secured the major towns and strategic points—airports, communication centers and military posts. Soviet soldiers, wearing long overcoats and gray fur caps with the red star insignia, huddled around fires or shelters carved from the mud and snow. Scores of empty tank transports parked by the roadside attested to the enormous firepower that now fanned out across the country. Some 300 tanks were in Kabul and the silhouettes of long-range artillery pieces speckled the snow-swept fields.

While armored vehicles and supply trucks poured in day and night, Antonov transports continued to land at the Kabul airport. By the end of the first week of January, 1980, more than 4,000 flights had been recorded.

Within weeks, at least 50,000 Soviet troops had arrived by land and air. This was in addition to the 4,000 civilian technicians and administrative advisors who had been brought in to "assist" the new Babrak Karmal administration.

Despite sporadic but intense fighting between the Soviets and the mujahideen guerrillas as well as rebellious Afghan military units, the mobility and numbers of the invaders took most people by surprise. In Kabul, people reacted with sullen disbelief and hostility, but except for shouts of abuse and stone throwing, there was little resistance. Moscow had chosen an opportune time of year to make its move. Western reaction to the invasion was dulled by the festive Christmas and New Year season. At this time of year Afghanistan was covered in snow and ice, severely limiting activities of the guerrilla resistance.

After securing the capital, the Soviets quickly adopted a low profile during daylight hours, but after dusk tanks rumbled through the streets to enforce the curfew.

By early January, spotty pockets of resistance began to form, particularly around Kandahar, Herat, and Jalalabad. Faced with an alarming rise in opposition from the Afghan army, the Soviets were obliged to effect controls over certain disloyal units or, as was the case with the 26th Afghan Parachute Regiment, suppress them with force.

Brutal reprisals followed each incident, but as much as possible, the Soviets sought to remain discreet and leave the Afghan authorities to deal with local problems whenever possible.

# CHAPTER 4

On Thursday, March 14, I awoke feeling vaguely ill and as we arrived at the Intercontinental Hotel to visit Stan, it hit! I was speaking with him from the phone in the lobby when suddenly I felt as if I were going to faint and lose sphincter control at the same time. I rushed to the front desk, but the haughty Pakistani desk clerk wouldn't direct me to the nearest rest room. Finally I found it on my own, almost too late, and exploded with diarrhea.

After this episode, I rested in the lobby and soon felt well enough to join Stan. As it turned out, he was also ill, so we postponed our meeting. Nasir challenged me to walk with him back to our hideout, about five miles away. I wanted to see something of the local area and it felt good to get outdoors and move about. However, severe abdominal cramps struck me again as we crossed a large intersection. I tried desperately to hail a taxi, wondering what local taboos would be violated by an American soiling himself in public. Allah was with us, because some friends of Nasir drove by in a van and rushed me home. I thought both ends would erupt en route, but held on, dripping sweat, and just made it to the bathroom for another explosion. Collapsing with fever and cramps, I lay around close to the toilet all afternoon. The diarrhea was so profuse that it dried up my runny nose! I must have lost five pounds in a few hours and my jeans were barely hanging on me by sundown. During the night peristalsis slowed. By the time of the mullah's morning call, I had fully recovered.

Friday, March 15, would be the most interesting day since my arrival. After a leisurely breakfast (only sweetened tea for me after the episode of the day before) I left with Nasir and Colonel Osmani to visit Dara, not far from Peshawar. For centuries this small hamlet (the name means valley) was proud of its legend: "Anything that money can buy, can be bought in Dara." Since the war started, guns and heroin had been the primary commodities. Anyone who entered Dara did so at his own peril. All law stopped at the village entrance. Outsiders, particularly Caucasians, were decidedly unwelcome unless they were dealing in drugs, guns or both. Nasir felt our visit would be a good test of my disguise as an Afghan. If I passed undetected there, I could safely visit other areas off limits to most Westerners. My beard had grown and I had to touch up the gray whiskers with mascara. My skin was browner now than it had been on my arrival, and my contacts were in place.

Our battered Suziki wound slowly down the rutted unpaved main street. We encountered nothing but hostile stares—not a friendly face, even from the usually obsequious proprietors of the roadside stalls. I felt very uneasy and stayed in the center of our group after we parked the Suzuki and began exploring the shops. Frequently craftsmen barred our entrance and rudely indicated we should pass on. Guns were everywhere—hand guns, automatic weapons, rifles, anti-aircraft cannons and mortars. Most were hand-made replicas, identical to the originals. The craftsmanship was remarkable. With only simple hand tools, pistols, rifles and even artillery pieces were manufactured from scrap iron, old railroad tracks, and lawn mower wheels. While I watched, one young man bored a precise rifle barrel out of a piece of railroad track using a hand auger.

Each shop and its occupant provided a scene worthy of *National Geographic*, but most merchants objected violently to any photographs. Even so, I was soon out of film. With Nasir translating, I had no problem buying all the film I wanted—even within the expiration date.

Colonel Osmani purchased a ball-point pen which fired a .22 cartridge and gave it to me as a souvenir. It is still a prized possession.

At tea time we entered a dark, crowded restaurant and sat far in the back to avoid attention. A large sheep slept next to our booth. In front of the shop, a meaty stew bubbled in a wok-like pot over an open fire, enticing us with the pungent aroma of curry. We sipped tea, and as I hesitantly nibbled on a cookie asked Nasir, "Are there raisins in your cookie?"

"Sure. Aren't some in yours?"

"I hope so. I was afraid I was eating flies."

Suddenly the proprietor walked up, snatched a huge curved knife from his robe and slashed the sheep's throat. Although blood gushed from the wound and the poor animal convulsed in its death throes, the event was ignored by everyone but me. The carcass was hung from a hook, skinned, gutted, and sectioned in a few minutes. Pieces were lopped off and tossed onto the grill or into the wok. The service here was bad, the cookies were worse, but no one could say this place didn't serve fresh meat—with an incomparable floorshow. The stew was as delectable as it smelled, so I ate my fill, sopping up the juices with delicious <u>nan</u>.

Full as ticks we returned to the safe house for another badminton tournament and the usual endless discussions. That morning I had tried to phone Pam. She returned my call while I was in Dara. I was afraid she would be worried when I wasn't there and finally got through to her. All was well at home, except Hayne had a cold. At 14 months he was just learning to walk, yet his vocabulary was amazing. It felt wonderful to talk to them, but our conversation made me homesick and discontented.

A new patient revived my spirits. One of the mujahideen leaders, Commander Babrakazay, asked me to treat his 88-year-old father. The old man looked as young as his son, but suffered from severe degenerative arthritis of both knees. I prescribed ibuprofen, a mild anti-inflammatory medication, and the old warrior returned my favor with a jar of dark honey. I was told it came from flowers of the high mountains and would help to ensure long life. I immediately began to use it in my tea.

After the trip to Dara and the evening's diplomacy, I was very tired but also excited. We were scheduled to leave for the border in one or two days.

On Saturday, March 16, I was alone all morning because everyone from our hideaway was busy with preparations for the trip. I sat, covered with flies, on the porch in the sun wrote a long letter to Pam and added to my notes about Afghan history and the Soviet invasion. I missed my family acutely and wished we would get on with the trip so I could return home. Our third wedding anniversary was only a month away. I would be a father again soon after that.

Dr. Bob Simon called in the early afternoon to tell us another American doctor and two nurses would be arriving within the week. Nasir returned, exhausted from all his preparations, and announced we were to leave for the border in the morning. No suitcases or backpacks were allowed, so I spent the afternoon trying to cram a sleeping bag, camera film, toiletries, morphine syrettes, various pills, socks and underwear into a small shoulder bag. As far as I could determine, I would be inside Afghanistan for about eight days, return to Peshawar, then go back inside again. I ended the evening by taking a long cold shower. There probably would not be another chance to be clean for some time.

Nasir and I left early for brunch at the Intercontinental Hotel with Stan, Emory, Dr. Daoud, and Dr. Nasraty. We should have eaten at home. The lettuce in my salad had the appearance and taste of wet tissue paper, while the scraps of radish were hot enough to sear my taste buds. There was no dressing to dilute the grit present in the salad, so I decided I wasn't that hungry and declined any more food, though I did sip the muddy coffee. I had learned to add lots of milk and sugar to slow the assault of its concentrated caffeine on my nervous system.

We discussed plans for our trip—a logistical nightmare because of all the camera equipment—and hoped to leave at the crack of dawn.

After meeting Stan and Emory, we drove to the house of Mr. Gailani, one of the political and religious leaders of the Afghan resistance. His home was cool, shaded by large trees and surrounded by frowning, heavily armed mujahideen. Mr. Gailani was a very gracious host, providing tea, sweets and a variety of video tapes of the Afghan struggle taken by British and French journalists.

One covered a battle involving a famous resistance leader, Ahmad Shah Massoud, and his band of warriors. Posters of Massoud were plastered all over Peshawar, but this was my first chance to see him "live." On tape he seemed to be in his 20s, handsome, and obviously very popular with his troops. Kindness and authority seemed to radiate from him as he directed the action. I was greatly impressed and hoped to meet him someday, but was told he never left his mountainous battleground or his followers in the Panjshir Valley.

After seeing the tapes, I was fired up for our trip, but my hopes were squashed again upon returning home. Nasir returned from a visit with some of the Afghan chieftains and told us all plans had been cancelled. He was obviously exhausted by all the negotiations.

The next morning our trip was on again, and we moved with our bags to Dr. Hashmet's house where we sat...and sat...and sat.

Just past noon the trip was again canceled. Apparently one of the Afghan tribal leaders had suffered hurt feelings when he wasn't asked about our plans and refused to provide support. On top of this, various dissenting tribesmen were stirring up things again. All afternoon Pakistani tanks and jets were roaring out of town toward the border. Something important must have been going on there.

Nasir was upset, I was upset, and everyone else seemed upset about the postponement. I'd had enough of eating, sleeping and waiting. With all the camera gear we would carry, plus medical supplies and at least ten people to be slipped across the border, I could understand the problems. But I wanted to get started doing what I had come to do: practice basic medicine in an exotic setting, and hopefully bring some semblance of medical care to these poor people.

Making Stan's documentary was vital. I knew it would provide much needed publicity for the Afghan cause; a subject American media seemed to ignore. I had no illusions the film would make me an instant celebrity or filmland's international sex symbol as Stan so frequently promised, his tongue fixed firmly in cheek.

If it were possible, I would have preferred to go with Nasir and a few mujahideen in a quick dash across the border to our destination.

The afternoon's lunch was light but delicious—rice, nan and bananas. This time carbonated soft drinks were served instead of tea. The local bottled products were sweet, almost to the point of syrup, and a poor tea substitute. By now I had grown to prefer sugary tea to any other drink. Slowly, I was becoming an Afghan.

After eating, we returned to our sanctuary for another afternoon of what had become ritual boredom. My ennui was partially relieved by experiencing a terrible time with my brown contact lenses. I couldn't insert them properly, but continued to work at it as I had nothing else to do aside from watching the endless badminton game.

After five or ten minutes of work I finally got the contacts in by myself and wore them all afternoon in celebration.

Nasir arrived to take me to another meeting with Stan and Emory at the Intercontinental Hotel. This time I was introduced to the bureaucracy necessary to get a beer.

First I had to produce my passport and prove I was a non-Muslim. After filling out a mimeographed sheet in triplicate detailing my age, nationality and reason for being in Pakistan, I was assigned a number, valid for one month. I had to produce this number in the hotel bar to obtain a few quarts of London beer, brewed in Pakistan and truly awful. Of course Nasir, being a Muslim, could not enter the bar. I was forced to stow the beer in a suitcase, take it outside and sit in the car to drink. Having lived in Germany, Nasir had tasted beer and willingly shared it with me. It was hardly worth the trouble, though I did derive some pleasure by annoying the rude desk clerk who thought I was a Pathan tribesman. He'd initially refused to talk to me or to recognize my passport, thinking I'd stolen it. Hooray, my disguise was working.

We choked down a few bottles of the horrible stuff before returning to the safe house for another big time badminton tournament. Dr. Osman won as usual.

Two visiting chieftains were not the typical tall, aquiline, skinny Afghans. These men, big as fullbacks, were leaders from villages in Paktia province where the first clinics were to be established.

One of them, Commander Hakim, wanted to make sure the first clinic was located in Palangay, his village. I was happy to agree and would have promised anything to these guys. They seemed very friendly, but God, I was glad they were on my side.

I was issued a hooded olive-drab field jacket donated by the Saudi Red Crescent Society—a very welcome addition to my kit, since I'd brought very little cold-weather gear.

The remainder of the afternoon was spent repacking for our trip, again scheduled for the next morning. We planned to cross the Afghan border into the southeastern province of Paktia. Apparently there was a great deal of Soviet air and artillery activity in the area but little ground fighting. This district was deemed relatively secure, and the local tribal commanders had agreed to welcome the establishment of clinics there.

Because of the badminton tournament, the crowd at our hideout had increased. Each bedroom was jammed with men engaged in volatile discussions. Mujahideen chiefs were praying in the living room. People were coming and going, banging the gate. The whole place was a madhouse. There were incessant calls for "*Khalifa.*" This poor man never knew whether two or twenty would appear for supper.

There was no opportunity for a shower. The possibility of an evening meal seemed very remote. The din continued. Afghans seem congenitally unable to whisper and all discussions were carried out at full volume. Late that evening the noise abated and I slept soundly.

# CHAPTER 5

In the early afternoon of Tuesday, March 19, after several unexplained delays, Stan, Emory, and I, accompanied by a dozen or more grim-faced Afghans piled into three battered Toyota pickups and left Peshawar for a butt-busting ride toward the town of Miran-Shah on the Afghan border.

At the main Pakistani checkpoint, guards hassled everyone and demanded substantial bribes to pass Stan and Emory. At first, they ignored me as I pretended to sleep in the back seat. Then one guard shook me awake, but I yawned in his face and closed my eyes again. He must have assumed this imperious manner belonged to an authentic Afghan and passed me through without questions. As we drove on, Nasir snapped a picture of me to celebrate the success of my disguise and performance.

"Nasir, I fooled them! I thought sure he was going to arrest me."

"No, Dr. Pres, now you look like a real Afghan."

I was very flattered. "*Tashakoor* (Thank you)."

"Yes," Nasir grinned. "You have a really big nose."

All afternoon we followed the winding hilly road southeast through country that reminded me of scenes from my favorite movie, "Gunga Din." A tall, fortress-like building capped each hilltop. As we descended into the valleys, our convoy scattered clusters of ragged people along the highway using little hammers to break rocks into small cubes repairing the roads as they had done for centuries. Near sundown we stopped for prayer, and then entered the crowded unpaved streets of Miran-Shah. My companions yelled and flaunted their weapons to clear the way.

This city was one of the primary supply and staging areas for the mujahideen. Trucks, camels, mules and horses laden with supplies moved slowly through the narrow dusty streets and headed for the Afghan border only a few kilometers away. Ragged, heavily armed troops with hostile eyes stared fiercely at our motorcade as we were hustled through the house of a local Afghan chieftain and bedded down on its flat roof.

A very restless night of sporadic gunfire, loud noises and animals bleating ended when a full bladder woke me before prayer call. I hurried

Disguised to cross the border into Afghanistan

through a quick breakfast of tea and *nan*, followed by the usual challenge of the contact lenses. This time Dr. Nasraty inserted them for me—to the amazement of the ever curious Afghans, laden with pistols, knives, and Kalashnikovs. Someone explained that the gunfire during the night, which sounded to me like a pitched battle, was only a "local disturbance."

I spent the morning sitting through endless jirgahs, not understanding a word. Nasir finally explained that more problems were developing because of the complicated arrangements needed for such a large group such as ours to sneak across the border. Adding to our difficulties, the Soviets had begun a new offensive near our destination, making travel in that area especially perilous.

Suddenly we were rushed into waiting vehicles shielded by armed Afghans and driven through the boisterous throng into a compound on the outskirts of town. Apparently too many people had taken note of our visit, so we had to go to a "secure location." Our group was concealed in an interior building within a walled fort surrounded by impassive armed guards. Another long wait, a huge meal, and then we three Americans were concealed in the canvas-covered back of a truck for the cross-country ride. At dusk the convoy halted at a small village near the border. We unloaded our gear into a storehouse and waited for camels to arrive.

Scads of cheerful curious children surrounded us. We played silly games with them while trying to ignore the ominous sounds of Soviet heavy artillery a few kilometers away.

By nightfall the bombardment had ceased, six camels were loaded and we began walking. Each camel carried about 700 pounds of food, ammunition and our camera equipment. They seemed to walk in slow motion but as I followed in line I realized they moved at a rapid pace. I also learned these beasts were odiferously flatulent.

We stumbled for miles through the dark in single file, following the bell of the lead camel up and down endless hills. Sometime after midnight we arrived at Zhawah, one of the main mujahideen staging areas just inside Afghanistan. Through the rest of the night troops were coming and going, walking, riding horses or driving small Toyota pickups. Dashika anti-aircraft gun pits encased by camouflaged sandbags perched on the hill tops surrounding the camp. Camels, horses and trucks mingled with bearded, turbaned soldiers carrying a variety of weapons. The whole place smelled of men, machines and animals—the stench of war.

Supplies and trucks were stored in camouflaged caves carved out of the hillside; these caverns also served as bomb shelters and camp latrines. (This hideout was the target of American Tomahawk missiles in 1998.)

I unrolled my sleeping bag on the floor of a large room packed with loud and curious Afghans. Many exhibited the unsettling custom of putting their faces right in mine, then staring for long minutes, much inside my "comfort zone." One of my contact lenses had slipped out; so with one blue eye and one brown, I attracted even more interest than usual. After the long day and long walk I was exhausted and went to sleep promptly in spite of the incessant loud conversations of these Afghan warriors.

In less than an hour I was awakened by explosive, profuse diarrhea and exited rapidly out the window to avoid stepping on the sleeping men. Hourly encores occurred throughout the rest of the night, and in the darkened latrine tunnel I soon had soiled my clothes. During brief intermissions I curled into a fetal position on my sleeping bag, cramping and sweating until dawn.

At earliest light I took off the shirt of my *kameez* and began washing it and myself with a bucket of water and some shampoo. In Afghan culture it is offensive for a man to be seen in public without a shirt, but my ablutions caused more amusement than offense, and the Afghans watched intently as Emory filmed my efforts to get clean.

We reloaded all our gear on the camels and moved out with a group of about 20 fighters. I hadn't realized how much the diarrhea had weakened me until we started up and down the interminable hills. Booming artillery echoed down the canyons, and our proximity to the war was emphasized as we met two fighters leading a camel down our narrow trail. A bed frame padded with blankets and lashed upside down on top of the camel held a pale, groaning Afghan. I examined him briefly and surmised his arm and chest wounds were so severe, he probably wouldn't live to reach Pakistan. I had no blood, antitoxin, antibiotics or intravenous fluids which might have saved him, but I was able to ease his pain with morphine and gave his companions additional syrettes to use as needed to keep the terribly injured man as comfortable as possible.

Once again I fumed from the frustration of knowing what to do and how to do it, but having no tools. This, unfortunately, would become a recurring theme. Over and over I was reminded, "To be wounded in Afghanistan is to die in Afghanistan."

My gastrointestinal problems continued. I became more dehydrated as the day passed, but hung on until early afternoon. When we finally stopped in a small village for a tea break, I collapsed. Fearing my weakened condition would slow us down, I lay on my prayer blanket as if asleep until they roused me, gulped enough sweetened tea to replace lost fluid volume until I could stand, then walk without fainting.

Our group pressed on through the mountains and met several hundred weary troops returning from the front lines wearing bandoleers of ammunition, large knives stuck in their belts, and carrying Kalashnikovs. Many were barefoot, clad only in rags, and obviously exhausted, but still they strutted along the trail. They were Afghans!

Some of these men wore tiny yellow flowers in their pockets, and one gave me an aromatic bouquet, then a fierce hug. Nasir translated that the man had been told I was an American doctor coming to help his people, and he wanted to welcome me to his country. This touching incident compensated for all the miseries thus far. Maybe my presence and caring would compensate for the meager medical assistance I could bring to these noble people.

Someone apparently had noted my dragging pace, for at the next village a horse was waiting for me. Because of unpleasant boyhood experiences, I have always intensely disliked horses, but my weakened condition outweighed my fear. I crawled aboard only to discover my mount was without bridle or saddle. My benefactors expected me to ride this nag bareback through the mountains at night! The infernal creature bucked and pitched for a time. I hoped Emory's camera wasn't recording my profanity. The way I looked and felt the film would need serious editing if I were to become the promised sex symbol.

We moved out and followed a steep, narrow trail, closer and closer to the rumble of artillery gunfire in the background. When we topped a sharp ridge, I could see Soviet tanks maneuvering in the valley below. Our little group moved cautiously through a deep canyon out of sight of the tanks, and in late afternoon paused at a hidden teahouse. These stops were increasingly welcome, for I was becoming weaker by the hour. The tea revived me to some extent and I struggled on. My Afghan companions never seemed to tire or grow thirsty.

Mohammed Arif, a male nurse going into a nearby village to set up a clinic, had walked alongside my horse all afternoon while I tried to teach him English. He was an apt student, repeating each phrase until he had it memorized. Once, as my horse lost its footing, reared and scattered rocks far in the canyon below, I yelled, "Oh, my God!" Mohammed dutifully repeated, "Oh, my God, Oh, My God, Oh, my God" until he had it right.

At dusk we entered a village high above a Soviet-infested plain that we would have to cross well after dark. When we walked down the main street, the booming voice of an Afghan greeted us, saying over and over, "Hello, hello, English persons! Welcome! Welcome! I speak pretty damn good English, you see."

This jolly man was a baker. He threw tortilla-sized pieces of dough against the wall of a heated pit where they stuck until toasted. Quickly snatching the golden bread out with a forked stick, he tossed it in the air to us. It was the most delicious nan I've ever tasted, fresh, hot and crusty. All the while, the baker kept up a continuous chatter of his few English expressions. I will always remember this village as the home of the "Happy Afghan."

His bread and tea having partially revived me, we set out to cross the dangerous plain.

It was so dark I could barely see my horse's head and the occasional black silhouettes of the *mujahideen*. No lights, cigarettes or conversation were permitted. Suddenly a search light swept back and forth across us. We froze and the light continued its rotation. I thought at first it was from a helicopter, and then realized it came from a Soviet outpost on the next hill.

We crouched in the shallow gully, hardly breathing. The light went out and we crept forward. In the darkness we stumbled upon another group of silent Afghans and everyone began shouting. The yelling and screaming continued for at least five minutes, while I huddled in the darkness expecting the searchlight to pinpoint us any second. But it didn't, and the noise stopped as abruptly as it began. We moved on. Nasir dropped back to inform me the other group had captured some collaborators and planned to shoot them on the spot. Our group had talked them out of it for fear the Soviets would hear the gunfire. Why they didn't hear the loud discussion I'll never know.

We moved on in the dark past several camel caravans traveling silently without bells or lights. No stars were out and I could make out only dim shapes in the distance. After three or four hours of steady walking, we re-entered the hills and our group relaxed. The artillery bombardment started again. We could see search lights crisscrossing the trail we'd just passed. Allah was with us.

Slowly and cautiously we climbed out of a deep canyon and entered a large pine forest infested with camels, horses and sleeping warriors. Sentries passed us through, and we settled by the embers of a small campfire concealed in a pile of boulders. By the time some feeling had returned to my numb posterior, tea was ready and the *nan* was warmed.

After this very welcome rest, we resumed our journey, following a winding, narrow path between towering black mountains. I prayed that my horse knew the trail and tried not to flinch when I heard rocks skittering off the trail to drop into a river far below.

About 2:00 a.m. we halted for the night and discovered that none of our gear, including my sleeping bag, had arrived. Apparently the horses had moved along the trail faster than camels carrying our supplies. I flopped onto the ground, wrapped myself in a filthy tattered blanket and went to sleep immediately.

All day my eyes had felt irritated even after removing the contacts. When I was awakened at daybreak by departing refugees, my eyelids were glued together. After forcing them apart, I stumbled into an empty hut and slept a few more hours. When we were reawakened by prayer call, and I was able to wash my eyes enough to be able to see through the narrow slits between my swollen lids.

I always seemed to look my worst when it was time to film, but I'd come to accept that I wasn't photogenic. My movie roles as a leading man would be limited.

Stan had already told me his documentary required no acting or script, just a record of daily activities. When they returned to California, he and Emory would construct a coherent story out of it. So I sat and talked to Nasir about the politics, his life before the war, and his hopes for the future, and tried to ignore the camera.

When walking alone or bouncing on the horse, I kept looking at pictures of Pam and Hayne. I missed them more with each passing day. Over and over I'd stare at the snapshots and drift into fantasies of holding them and telling Hayne stories of Daddy's Afghan adventure. We were just starting our journey, and already I was terribly homesick.

It was the 21st of March, the first day of spring and the Afghan New Year, which explained the ubiquitous yellow flowers carried by the troops we'd met the day before. I presumed the flowers symbolized new hope for them in their struggle. If nothing else the tiny blossoms brought a touch of beauty to the harsh realities of war.

I prayed this New Year would be a better one for these people of nature. They certainly deserved liberty and were willing to fight for it. As one of them told me the previous day, "The only superpower we fear is Allah."

What devout and courageous people. With these thoughts I felt somewhat stronger, my eyes were better, and I realized I was now far inside Afghanistan, hungry, missing my family but having the adventure of my life.

On the same plodding, fractious horse, I moved over the tortuous mountain trails, frequently meeting small bands of tired warriors returning from the front lines. These men had already marched over 200 miles and looked to be in much better shape than we were. Most of them were small soldiers with an Asian cast to their features, wearing old leather shoes, torn sandals, or no shoes at all. These troops seemed in good spirits, but ours dampened when we passed the rotting carcasses of five or six camels amid the deep bomb craters scattered over the barren hills. I was told this was the site of a helicopter gunship attack only a few days earlier on a supply train. The odor of decay spoiled my appetite, but hot tea was always welcome. We crowded into a mud hut to sit out a sudden rain shower.

Our trail wound across mountain slopes stripped completely bare from centuries of deforestation and dotted every few hundred yards with abandoned charcoal ovens. There was no cover from aircraft, so this was a very dangerous area, particularly since we were approaching a large Soviet encampment.

I felt extremely vulnerable sitting exposed on horseback, and would have been more than happy to walk. My horse had trotted uncontrolled for miles, and my butt was in agony. We topped one more peak which overlooked a beautiful village near a wide stream which bisected large wheat fields. I would also have liked to stop and admire the spectacle of our caravan wending its way across this ancient land, but we were in full view of a sandbagged Soviet outpost on a hilltop nearby. When we zigzagged down the slope into the fields, the Soviet soldiers watching us closely through their binoculars seemed strangely unconcerned with our progress. More curious than menacing, perhaps they too were drawn to the timeless pageantry. Our guides, however, were very nervous. This outpost, I learned, was known to fire mortars at transients, sometimes just to see them jump.

Just as I had feared, my horse balked right in the middle of the most exposed area. Even though I almost kicked his ribs in, the stubborn animal refused to budge. Since he hadn't responded to my large vocabulary of American cuss words, I tried a few words of Pashto— "*Rasha! Rasha!* (Come on) *Mundah!, Mundah!* (Run, run)"

No use. I dismounted and began kicking and pulling while the Soviets watched intently. I couldn't hear the comments, but I'm sure the horse and I provided their entertainment for the day. At least they were amused enough not to lob a mortar shell to put me and that blasted animal out of our misery.

I finally got him going, made it through the stream, and into the relative security of a small canyon. Soon our trail became so narrow and steep I had to dismount and lead the horse past several camel caravans that had settled down for the night. The poor beasts knelt in place with their loads left on, and their folded legs were wrapped with a rope so they couldn't stand up. It looked terribly uncomfortable, but the camels sat placidly chewing, obviously unconcerned about the strenuous climb awaiting them in the morning.

After dark, we entered the village of *Billar* (Afghan for barrel; named for the barrels of asphalt used to surface the road) on the highway from Khost to Kabul. This village was occupied early on by the Soviets soon after the invasion, but the *mujahideen* later recaptured it, as well as all its asphalt barrels, which they'd used to make bunkers and houses.

While we rested, I realized that for the past 48 hours I had eaten nothing except some tough beef jerky. But at least my intestinal symptoms had ceased, and I felt stronger although extremely grungy. I smelled awful and my hair was a matted tangle too dirty to comb. My clean clothes were packed with the medicines on the camel caravan - wherever that might be.

After tea the usual loud discussions commenced but mercifully lasted only a short time. I'd settled down for a good night's sleep but was jolted awake by a large cat jumping on my face. After this shock I composed myself and was again dozing when I realized a mouse had taken refuge in my sleeping bag. He exited promptly, probably gagging from the odor, with the cat in hot pursuit.

Even with these interruptions it was the most restful night for me since leaving Peshawar. By morning I felt completely well. The Afghans and I drank tea and dozed while we waited for camels, trucks, or some form of transportation.

Suddenly I heard the ominous "Whomp, Whomp, Whomp," of approaching helicopters, and two Soviet MI-24/HINDs materialized, apparently following the road to Khost. These monsters looked as if some drunken welder had built them in his back yard. Rockets, gun barrels and all sorts of things were hanging off the sides. The monstrous aircraft seemed to stay aloft only by beating the air into submission. Their ungainly appearance made them all the more formidable. At least their deafening noise warned us in time to run.

"*Beelah, beelah, putsha* (hurry, hide yourself)," the Afghans yelled.

Like BB's on a hardwood floor, we scattered into a grove of trees bordering a terraced, irrigated field.

I was well hidden in a deep ditch, and except for the helicopters it was an extremely peaceful scene. In the warm sun I relaxed and tried to enjoy the feeling, but the deafening noise reminded us that we were in the midst of war. I could see the pilots leaning out of their armored seats to peer at us, but they demonstrated no hostile interest in our group. The aircraft had hardly disappeared when Afghan wood choppers nonchalantly resumed their task of hewing massive beams from felled trees, then loading the lumber on two camels.

We piled into an old captured Soviet truck and inched along the highway past mounds of twisted armored cars and vehicles littering both sides of the road. Enemy reconnaissance planes and gun ships passed over every few minutes. When they appeared, we would hide in the woods for a brief time, then resume our journey. It was obvious we must get away from this area soon.

Our progress was halted by a sudden violent argument between rival chiefs and their followers. This unrest had been brewing during the entire trip and now exploded. Apparently issues involved the prestige of each group, questions regarding the distribution of supplies and the order of visits to various villages. The matter was finally settled with only low-grade grumbling for the next few hours.

We continued our trek along the road, our path littered with wrecked tanks, armored personnel carriers and the detritus of a furious battle.

I asked how the *mujahideen* were able to stop these armored vehicles with only rifles. While we traveled, a story was recounted to me which increased my respect for the Afghans and their struggle against seemingly overwhelming odds.

Initially, I was told, the freedom fighters would run up to the tanks and fire through the gun ports to kill the drivers. But they were losing a lot of their own men that way. One day a large bomb, dropped from a Soviet warplane, failed to explode. The Afghans rolled it beneath a bridge and, not knowing how to detonate it, built a fire under it. The resulting explosion blew up the bridge. The Afghans then disguised the cavity with mats. The next Soviet tank naturally fell into the hole and the *mujahideen* killed the occupants. As the battle raged, women and children were sent out from the village with rocks to knock the lugs off the turret bolts. The men remove the cannon and used it against the oncoming vehicles. Who could defeat such ingenuity and courage?

Later, we passed a disabled tank in which a Soviet soldier and two communist Afghans had been trapped for three days. The three soldiers were out of water and out of hope, yet they still refused to leave. Obviously they couldn't escape, but the *mujahideen* couldn't get to them either. Finally hunger and thirst overcame fear, and the occupants came out of the tank to surrender. Naively I asked, "Did you shoot them then?"

"No," the Afghan chieftain cheerfully replied. "We talked to them awhile, and then we shot them."

All the battered vehicles we saw on the roadside had been stripped of everything usable and were marked with various symbols and graffiti which were translated to me as anti-Soviet slogans and messages of hope to the Afghan people.

After a brief stop for tea was spent in the small village of Mirajan, we bounced over a rutted rocky road, then up a stream bed toward Commander Hakim's village of Palangay. Our truck ground along in the lowest gear as we crawled by bubbling springs that watered terraced fields and apricot trees in full bloom. Large apartment-like adobe houses clung haphazardly to the slopes.

Every few minutes our old truck would stall and die. Our driver would get out, use a hand air pump to clear the carburetor, and the engine would sputter back to life. At each puddle we'd stop to refill the radiator. I could have easily walked to our destination faster than we were going, but I was happy to stand in the back of the truck instead of placing my sore buttocks on the back of a horse. The stubborn old nag had disappeared. I hoped it had been eaten by the tribesmen.

When we entered Palangay, Afghan men lined the streambed and silently watched while women and children peered through half-shuttered windows.

Hakim's village was spectacular. It was full of terraced gardens, lush orchards, and sprawling vineyards. Long aqueducts paralleled the streambed. There was even a primitive water mill for grinding wheat. The apartment-like clay-and-timber homes were daubed with pastel colors. Snow-covered mountains in the background framed by a brilliant blue sky completed this picture post-card scene.

The truck wheezed to a stop and the air around us exploded. I later learned it is an Afghan custom that when an honored guest enters a village all the defenders guns are fired in salute. The prestige of each village is demonstrated by its firepower. I have to admit, though, that when over a hundred armed men on either side of me raised their weapons and began yelling, I thought my trip was truly at an end.

Commander Hakim barked an order and the village fell silent. Another order and I jumped as the 50 caliber anti-aircraft gun above us on the hillside began its bam-bam-bam, joined by the earsplitting crackle of rifles, Kalashnikovs and a few ancient shot guns. Hot shell casings flew everywhere, a smoky haze obscured the village, and the strong smell of gunpowder settled over me. Still the firing continued, for we were among the first Americans to visit Palangay, and we were to be impressed. Ammunition seemed to be unlimited. The onlookers cheered lustily, and the celebration continued for nearly half a minute until silenced by another signal from Commander Hakim. He hugged each of us in turn and kissed our cheeks while the villagers swarmed over our gear, not allowing us to carry anything. The smoke and echoes disappeared, and I felt like a conquering hero when I walked up the steep hillside and entered the coolness of a shadowy whitewashed room.

While we relaxed on large cushions surrounding beautiful carpets, *hors d'oeuvres* were served—*nogul* (a delicious candy), *nan*, and steaming rice. After three days of nothing but jerky I was finally able to eat decent food.

After the meal I felt great and taped an interview with Stan, mostly reading from my journal. As the light faded, Emory filmed me writing in my notebook. I looked forward to getting a good night's sleep after many restless ones in the past. The sunset was fantastic. High over the mountains billowy rain clouds hovered, filtering the last few rays of the dying red sun. What a beautiful place. I wished we could extend our time in Palangay, but I knew we had to go on to another village soon. Any foreigner stopping for more than a couple of days created a dangerous risk. Word of the visit would leak out, followed by bombing or more severe reprisals.

But this evening made the whole trip worthwhile, and as I said for the cameras, "If I didn't have a wife and family, I would stay here forever."

My euphoria of the evening carried through the night with a wonderful dream—in living color. I was starring in a movie called "The Towers of Rawalpindi" and of course was the hero, with looks and physique of Douglas Fairbanks, Jr. Such are the tricks the mind can play when a person is under stress.

I awoke in excellent humor and began to explore the area. Our horses and camels hadn't arrived with the medicines, so I couldn't start the clinic as planned. Nasir left early to retrace our route and locate the supplies.

I stood gazing out over the valley, watching horsemen traveling along the mountain ridges, listening to the sounds of roosters crowing, donkeys braying and the pleasant gurgling of the stream. How peaceful—an illusion abruptly destroyed by Russian jets suddenly blasting overhead. I dove into a bombed-out house as they shot overhead and prayed lightning really didn't strike twice in the same place. The village guns roared for a time—probably in frustration—then all went quiet except for the pleasant sounds I had enjoyed before the intrusion. The smoke cleared and everyone was smiling, obviously relieved no bombs had fallen. Once again the war had spared us for a time.

I spent the rest of the morning wandering about and exploring the primitive aqueducts. For some reason these rustic structures fascinated me. From high mountain streams water coursed through hand-built ditches, ran over and under rocks, around slopes, always at the proper angle to ensure a controlled flow. As best I could determine, these waterways continued to be built today as they had been for centuries, one rock at a time. The village engineer used a hollow tube filled with water, markings on the tube determining the proper slope for the canals. With this crude device the precise angle of declination was determined. What patience and dedication it must have taken to construct such systems—but these are typical Afghan characteristics.

# CHAPTER 6

In the afternoon we joined a group of villagers on a nearby hillside for target practice. A small hand mirror was placed on an adjacent ledge about a hundred yards away and we took turns firing at it. Everyone missed. Then an ancient Afghan with a face like parchment and a vintage rifle strode over, fired nonchalantly and hit the mirror dead center. Everyone heartily cheered his skill, and we returned to the village at the end of a delightful day.

As we lay on our mats, Quadrat Nasraty and I dissolved in laughter as we mimicked various groups attempting to speak English - black, Pakistani, Arabian, Texan, and even South Carolinian. Then we re-enacted old Hollywood harem B-movies with dialogue like "Bring me the English woman!" and "I was locked in the tower by my uncle, who seized my father's throne."

Quadrat was a wonderful companion, splendid with voices and dialects.

I wished he could someday visit us in Texas. With his good looks, intelligence, surgical skills and sense of humor, he would be an instant hit anywhere.

Monday, March 25, proved to be a very eventful day, though it began with a lazy morning as I wandered around looking at the scenery, examining captured weapons and talking with Quadrat. Just before noon our group assembled to depart for a settlement three to four miles away. This detour was to be primarily diplomatic rather than medical, designed to bolster the honor of their village chieftain, who wanted to be able to claim a visit from the American doctor.

Not to be outdone by the firepower of Palangay, we were greeted with cannons, rifles, Kalashnikovs and exploding land mines. The land mine was certainly an interesting touch we hadn't encountered in previous welcomes. The premature explosion of one mine, however, almost did away with the demonstrator as well as their honored guests. Rather than show alarm, our hosts simply laughed it off.

We were ushered into a large banquet room and seated on cushions for a sumptuous feast. Just when we began eating, I noticed an Afghan on my far left reaching for some food with a gargantuan hand. He leaned forward and I saw under his black turban the typical coarsened facial features of acromegaly.

A cold shiver ran down my spine as I recalled the dream I'd had before leaving home. I turned to Doctor Osman seated on my right and said, "That man has acromegaly." He replied, as I knew he would, "He does, he does."

Shaken, I then told him of my dream. He dismissed it with a shrug. "It's only déjà vu."

Everything was so exact that I was sure I remembered dreaming it. I made a mental note to ask Pam about the dream when I returned.

The meal was naturally followed with a lengthy post-banquet discussion. Understanding nothing, I could only smile and nod. I'd done my part, made an appearance and hopefully created some new friends.

After the ritual hugging and kissing, we began the winding trek back to Palangay. Since I was the guest of honor I was coerced into riding the community's only horse. We had traveled only a few miles before stomach cramps and nausea recurred, but the Afghans would not let me dismount. Each time I would try, they shook their heads and held my legs on both sides of the horse. All too soon my control failed, and I soiled myself, the horse and surely my honored status. After that, they gave no argument on letting me walk.

When we crossed a shallow stream, I let the others walk ahead while I cleaned up as best I could. By the time we reached Palangay, the sun was going down. Stan began yelling for me to come up and film the final scene of my clinic work before the light faded. Nasir had returned. He'd backtracked our route and found our camel caravan resting and awaiting further instructions. After an intense jirgah, he got them going. Now, with our supplies having finally arrived, we set up the clinic for the sick who were already lined up.

I begged for a little more time to clean up, but this was Stan's last chance to film the scene, so I donned an old fatigue jacket and began examining patients. Maybe they were used to the smell, but I certainly wasn't. Yet somehow we made it through. Afterwards Stan joked that I should receive a special Academy Award for the best performance by an actor who had just crapped in his costume.

Cameras, film and equipment were packed into an old Russian truck and I said good-bye to Stan and Emory as they left for the border.

Nasir, Quadrat and I joined a small group of local Afghans to hike through the night to another settlement. I felt strong, even after the day's

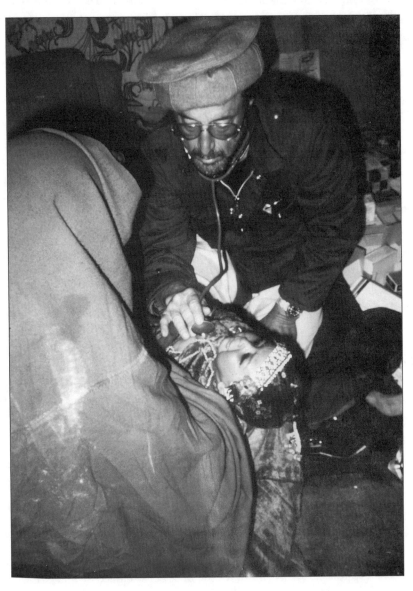

Clinic Day

events, so we set a brisk pace over the hills for three hours until we entered a long valley. On each of the opposing hilltops a huge guard dog was chained. Their loud barking at our approach alerted the village. We fired off a few shots to identify ourselves, the shots were answered, and we entered the friendly village of Surikiel about midnight.

Nasir made my needs known, and I was furnished a basin of water which I promptly took to the animal pens in the lowest level of an adobe split-level house, stripped off and cleaned myself as best I could. While my clothes were washed, I dressed in pants and a field jacket I'd borrowed from Nasir. I resolved not to eat anything the following day, laid down on a pallet on the roof and fell asleep immediately.

Rest ended abruptly at dawn. All the village guns began firing, whether in celebration, anger or defense I never knew. After only tea for breakfast, I set up a small clinic and was rapidly seeing patients when I discovered the crate on which I sat contained land mines. More such boxes were stacked all around me. I guess they figured the safest place for me to work would be in their armory, but the environment certainly helped me work efficiently and reduced waiting time to a minimum.

I saw about fifty patients in two hours, mainly with symptoms of worms, malnutrition and "various aches and pains," as their complaints were translated to me. The language barrier slowed our progress, but I soon found I could communicate with a few words, sign language and Nasir's help.

My "medical supplies" consisted of pills varying in size and colors, mostly vitamins of German origin, all well past their expiration date. These were tumbled together as if obtained from doctors who were cleaning out their sample drawers.

I did have a meager supply of antibiotics which was soon exhausted, and several gallons of vile-tasting cough medicine I used as a general tonic for all ailments.

One of my last patients was a feeble old Afghan wearing glasses as thick as coke bottles. He walked supported by a stick imbedded in a battered flashlight. From the attitude of the villagers, I could tell this elder was particularly loved and respected, so I asked Nasir to tell me about him.

During the battle for this village a few years before, the Soviets had been so well hidden down in the valley that Afghan snipers couldn't pick them off. This ancient one approached the snipers and said, "I'm old. I've lived my

The hero of his village

life. Give me a gun and I will go down and challenge them to surrender. When they shoot me, watch closely where they are firing from and you can pick them off."

The patriarch took the proffered rifle, made his way down into the middle of the settlement, stood his ground and challenged them to surrender. Unbelievably all twelve gave up. He escorted the prisoners back to his friends, forever after a hero. The Soviets obviously respected and feared these brave Afghans, regardless of age.

Patients seemed genuinely appreciative that something was being done for them, that someone from outside cared. Their hugs and smiles were more than adequate payment. I would accept this type of "fee for service" anytime.

When the morning concluded, we prepared to leave. Overall, I felt I'd made many friends and paved the way for those to follow.

In early afternoon we left Surikiel, walking fast. The chieftain's son stayed with us for about three miles then paused to say good-bye to his father before returning home. Both men were tearful, unusual in Afghan males, but this was a particularly poignant departure. We'd learned earlier that the Soviets might attack Surikiel in a few days. When I realized Commander Hakim had left his village and his son just to get us out safely, I also burst into tears. I thought no one noticed, but later in the day Nasir confided how touched he was that I wept for his people.

After walking for about another hour, we were suddenly pelted by a violent hailstorm and took cover under nearby trees. Nasir and I gathered some of the grape-sized hailstones in his <u>patoo</u> and ate them, for I knew this would be safe water. The icy treat was so refreshing I welcomed the hail and asked Nasir the Pushto word for it. "<u>Jala</u>." He pronounced it "shala," a beautiful sound and a wonderful girl's name. I vowed if Pam's baby was a girl, <u>Jala</u> would be her Afghan nickname.

The hailstorm lasted only five or ten minutes, stopped as abruptly as it started—rather like our spring storms in West Texas—and we resumed our journey. Nasir was far ahead of me when we reached a collection of abandoned buildings surrounding a rustic mill powered by an ancient water wheel. A little girl sat by the stream, her face covered by a lacy blue veil. We had been warned repeatedly not to take pictures or even look at the women, but when I passed by the child turned, dropped her veil, and I looked into the face of the most enchanting young girl I had ever seen. She turned away in an instant and I walked on. But her dark eyes and perfect features were burned into my mind forever. Many months later I saw the cover photograph on <u>National Geographic</u> of a strikingly beautiful Afghan girl, but even she did not compare with my vision.

Some to whom I have told this story have suggested I must have seen an angel, and I certainly would not dispute them. I shall never forget her.

We continued our hectic pace through flat muddy fields until we reached a highway of sorts, honeycombed with shell holes and lined with wrecked tanks and armor. Nasir, Quadrat, Col. Osmani, Commander Hakim and I packed into a small Toyota pickup with an Afghan driver who possessed the loudest voice and the most incredible body odor I'd yet encountered. I was squeezed into the middle of the front seat so there was no escape. Rain poured down, and his tape player blasted God-awful music. I told Nasir it sounded as though they had someone trapped inside a metal garbage can who was beating on the sides with sticks and screaming to be let out. He merely smiled.

All Afghans drive as if the devil was chasing them, and this gentleman was no exception. He made the Toyota do tricks that would easily qualify him as a Hollywood stunt driver. With Allah's protection we finally arrived—skidding, sliding, wet, cold and exhausted—in the town of Billar we'd left two days before. It had been severely bombed since then; fortunately there had been no deaths.

Tomorrow the precipitous hike toward Peshawar would begin.

My sleeping bag was relatively dry, though everything else was soaked, and the night passed no worse than usual. Early the next morning we started for home. I rode another anti-American nag up the mountain following a steep narrow trail through a series of switchbacks. The horse faltered before we were halfway to the summit, and I was forced to walk again. As we ascended, I passed through a layer of clouds so distinct my head and shoulders were clear above while my feet were hidden below. I turned and watched a camel's head emerge from the mist, then the body slowly appear as if it were surfacing from under water.

The ascent continued through a frigid rain shower which changed to drumming hail as we struggled up the sodden trail. We reached the summit cold and soaked to the skin, then stumbled through more hail and rain to the valley below. My fatigue magically disappeared when we slogged past an abandoned Soviet outpost. At least this time I wasn't slowed by a balky horse.

At a one-room teahouse concealed in the dense woods the hot syrupy beverage partially revived my body and spirits.

During this break I treated a boy with a badly infected eye, who was very grateful; then an ancient hostile Afghan demanded my jacket and was quite offended when I refused to give it to him. Just like at home—you can't please everybody.

We pressed on, up a grade so steep my eyes were on a level with the rear end of the man in front of me. As my pace slowed I was pulled along by an Afghan holding one end of my prayer blanket while I clutched the other. Hakim pushed and pulled me much of the way. Later, I gave him my Swiss army knife to repay his kindness. Soon even the Afghans were tired, and I began to suffer episodes of vertigo relieved only by frequent pauses for rest. My big toes were becoming increasingly painful, but I didn't have time to take off my boots to examine them.

We staggered through a blinding rain and were met by a young boy leading a horse, which Nasir had sent back for me. I was ashamed to ride when everyone else was mired in mud, so we loaded some of our gear onto the horse and squished along beside it. The rain became a torrent. We passed the site of the dead camels and began sliding down the mountain to ford icy, knee-deep streams. Dripping and miserable, we gathered in a small shepherd's hut, cold, wet and famished. Some *partially* boiled eggs were offered, but I decided I wasn't quite that hungry. All my jerky was gone, and I hadn't brushed my teeth for two days. Hail rattled down, beating its way through the thatched roof. Ignoring the weather, the Afghans spent an hour talking, eating and praying, while I squatted by the fire in the dark, trying to dry out and get warm. Pungent steam rose from our clothes and mingled with the acrid smoke.

The low-pitched babble of another incomprehensible conversation exerted a hypnotic effect. I stared into the flames, and then looked up into the shadowy, bearded faces of the tribesmen. A sense of unreal wonder filled my soul. The barn-loft dreams of my youth, fantasies of exotic adventure, had finally come true. I was wet, cold and hungry, but I was supremely content. Zen-like, I had become one with the Afghan tribesmen.

I would have been happy to stay in the damp hovel until the weather eased, but Nasir said we must walk six more hours before dark. The torrential rain and hail continued. We trudged along while I used all my mental tricks to keep going, mostly singing and reciting poems to myself. "The Shooting of Dan

McGrew" was a particular favorite. I tried to remember the second verse of the Star Spangled Banner, and so forth until we reached the village of the "Happy Afghan."

We'd crossed the soggy plain, this time at least free from Russian searchlights and patrols. The weather was too bad even for our enemies. No Happy Afghan or other villagers were seen, so about thirty of us bedded down in a large barn. During the night one of the Afghans began screaming and writhing about until Dr. Osman somehow calmed him down. Later I learned the poor man was suffering from "war nerves."

Morning began with the indescribable joy of not suffering from the runs, the first time in many days. Struggling through mud on the back of another nag, I finally reached the summit of the next mountain. Going down, I felt safer walking and leading the stubborn horse. All was going well. I was keeping up with the Afghans and congratulating myself that I'd at last become trail-hardy. Long before we reached the next valley, however, my big toes grew so painful I could barely walk. I limped into the headquarters at Zhawar late in the evening and was finally able to take off my ill-fitting boots. Both big toes had hemorrhaged under the nails, tearing them from their beds. I taped them back on as best I could, and squeezed out the blood so I could walk. Thank God the old Suzuki jeep was still safely hidden in a cave. We piled aboard for the long trip back to Miran-Shah and then to Peshawar through a continuous downpour of rain mixed with hail. About ten miles past Miran-Shah Commander Hakim told our driver to stop. He got out and instructed the driver to proceed on. I was confused. Wasn't he going on to Peshawar with us? Nasir then told me Hakim had left his village and came through the past three days of hell simply to make sure I was safe. Now he would walk back home. What a friend! What an Afghan! Would I ever see him again to thank him?

The Afghans asked me to drive so they could sleep. Their confidence in my driving skills through the traffic of Pakistan was sadly misplaced. I zoomed through the monsoon steering with my right hand, shifting gears with my left, driving on the left side of the road and dodging trucks. Somehow they managed to snore blissfully through a couple of visits into ditches and one complete donut in the mud. But Allah protected us. We reached Peshawar.

As usual there was no water at the safe house, but Dr. Osman let me borrow his room at the "lavish" Galaxy Hotel. I was able to take a shower, write a few cards home, and then sleep. I had been "inside," become an Afghan, and survived.

# CHAPTER 7

After a warm shower and a good night's sleep, I was well rested but awoke too early again and was forced to sit in the hotel lobby several hours waiting for a ride to our Peshawar hideout, time enough to review the recent journey and any achievements thus far. Medically I had accomplished little, despite my earlier hopes of bringing substantial medical care to the Afghans.

Although I had equipped three clinics and left them staffed by Afghan medics, I could do nothing to alleviate the appalling sanitary conditions. It didn't do much good to treat a child for worms if he worked in fields used for the village latrine. It did no good to treat an Afghan's bronchitis when he returned each night to a smoke-filled hut. Nothing I could do would help the nervous condition of a 16-year-old mother of two whose husband would never return from the war. At least, though, an American presence was established in this war-ravaged land, and maybe word would pass through the country's grapevine that an American doctor was interested in their plight and trying to help. For me, it was better than sitting at home wringing my hands or writing a check to some nebulous refugee foundation so I could blot the problem from my conscience.

Shortly before noon, my friends arrived, and I returned to the safe house to bid farewell to Stan and Emory. They wanted to film one more scene of me looking at pictures from home, so they shot a brief segment while I examined the well-worn photographs of Pam and Hayne.

Emory, Stan and I exchanged promises to meet in Sacramento for the movie's premiere, which I hoped would help the Afghan cause more than my meager medical efforts had so far. Of course I asked Stan to phone Pam when he returned to the States so she would know I was alive and well.

Pam and I had been warned that "bad people" in the U.S. might call her saying I had been killed or captured, or would try to get information about our activities in Afghanistan. So I had to give Stan a code to identify himself to Pam. On the mantel in our living room were brass dolphins. I told Stan to mention these to Pam and she would know he truly knew me.

Several months later Stan told me how aloof and hostile Pam had been when he called, until he said, "Pres asked me to tell you, 'Polish the dolphins'." Then her outburst of questions almost melted the telephone.

Half a world away from home, I met the new medical personnel sent by Dr. Simon. Jane Orlando, a charming lady from Dallas, was an operating room nurse who brought considerable experience and professional skills. Originally from Tennessee, Diane Price was also a highly trained nurse who kept a detailed journal and planned to write a story of their adventures. Harvey Snyder was a very friendly but somewhat strange physician from Ohio, tall and slim with a gray Lincolnesque beard, who seemed obsessed with religion. He prayed rather ostentatiously before each meal and apparently viewed his mission as an attempt to bring Christianity to the heathen rather than helping the ill and wounded. I sensed the Afghans were more puzzled than offended by Dr. Snyder's behavior, at least for the present. During the lazy afternoon all of us talked about our backgrounds and what we hoped to accomplish while in Afghanistan.

A group of local Afghan doctors had asked me to write an article for their medical publication discussing my recommendations to improve medical care in Paktia. I agreed, although I was a little concerned about causing offense if I spoke my mind openly. In my judgement, their greatest health risk was not the lack of modern medicines, but rather the atrociously low standards of hygiene and sanitation and the absence of any preventive health measures.

Since we had no water or electricity, everyone went to bed early, but I lay awake composing the article and worrying about the delay in starting my next trip. I'd planned to be away from home only a month, and three weeks had already passed. The next morning slipped by as I drank tea, swatted flies and worked on the article.

After lunch, Nasir and I went to the Intercontinental Hotel and used my documents to buy beer, then took it to his tiny apartment for a long, rather tearful discussion about his life, his ex-wife and son who lived in Germany and his longing for them. It was good therapy for both of us, but Afghans at our "headquarters" were very upset by Nasir's condition on our return. I suspected his mission was to loosen my tongue with a little alcohol and make sure I was not an assassin, CIA agent, or someone who would be a risk to them before they made any future plans for me. I could have told Nasir he was certainly my master at climbing mountains or hiking, but he had met his match when drinking beer.

Apparently a dangerous mission was being planned, possibly involving a foray into the Panjsher Valley, the site of constant fighting between Massoud's forces and the Soviets. Most of their discussion involved my qualifications and ability to survive a trip through the formidable Hindu Kush mountains.

Later that evening, Hakim and many of the village commanders from Paktia arrived for dinner. I had feared I would never see them again, so we shared hugs, kisses and attempts to communicate. Harvey and the nurses were busy getting ready for their trip. I wasn't told what I would be doing next—going with the nurses, going in alone, or returning to the States. I went to bed hoping some decision would be made soon.

Again I awoke before dawn. I should be a good Muslim as I was always wide-awake for morning prayer calls. Since there wasn't any water or electricity inside the house, I brushed my teeth at a spigot in the yard. The day started as usual with badminton and tea, then Nasir and I took Diane and Jane downtown to shop. I also wanted to pick up some pictures I'd left to be developed. Most of them were ruined by the processor, but the few surviving snapshots of Pam and Hayne made me more homesick than ever. I spent the afternoon leafing through the photos and trying to clean up a little for the large dinner that was planned.

Late that evening we were joined by Ms. Karen McKay, a vivacious director of the Committee for a Free Afghanistan, who was touring the refugee camps. Her enthusiasm was infectious, but I feared it would be dulled by frustrations of battling disease, poor sanitation and restrictive Muslim customs. However, she could at least report the appalling conditions to those in the United States who might help us make things better.

The tedium of the next morning was pleasantly relieved by a delicious luncheon with Mr. Gailani and his family, followed by videotapes of British sitcoms. One of their favorites was "Watch Your Language" about a group of foreign students attempting to learn English. Dr. Nasraty's routine during our stay in Palangay had been much funnier.

We returned to our sanctuary for a long meeting with several commanders from Paktia who were trying to make arrangements for the nurses' trip. Dr. Bob Simon called and seemed upset that I wasn't making preparations for a return to Paktia with Jane and Diane. Bob was very much opposed to the proposed journey into the Panjshir Valley, saying it was far too dangerous and would likely result in my being killed or captured. Such an event could ruin the future of the International Medical Corps and embarrass the United States government.

As a family man I was naturally very concerned with my safety, but reminded Bob plans for the trip were moving fast, and we should make an immediate decision. I would go if it would significantly help the Afghans, but for no other reason. I wanted to return to the U.S. if the Panjshir trip was canceled. Giving the phone to Nasir, I left the room so he and Bob could discuss the situation. Soon after their conversation, Massoud's brother arrived and I was invited into one of the bedrooms for an interview. Nasir served as interpreter. I was grilled at length and quickly determined they were trying to decide if I would be physically able to withstand the rigors of the journey. They also had to make sure I was not an assassin or double agent. Their occasionally heated discussion continued for a long time after I was dismissed.

Eventually Nasir joined me and said that Massoud would be contacted to see if he would approve our trip. The plan involved a trek of at least ten days to reach the Panjshir Valley, a week spent with the rebel leader, then our return. Nasir again stressed the difficulties of the trip, emphasizing that he himself had never been in the area of our proposed route. He reiterated we would undoubtedly suffer from the terrain, Soviet action and hostility from mountain tribesmen whose only allegiance was to Allah. To avoid discovery we would have to shun the usual trails and stay high in the Hindu Kush Mountains. (Hindu Kush means "Hindu Killer" as so many Indian troops had died trying to cross these mountains in past wars.)

Since the terrain was so challenging, we could carry very few supplies and hope to buy food as we traveled. Any more details would await Massoud's decision. I would decide whether or not to go after we had received his approval and I'd discussed it with Pam. Apparently Nasir had already convinced Bob Simon we should make the trip.

The water supply at our house was briefly restored, so I took a quick cold shower and changed clothes. People were constantly coming and going as plans for the trip were discussed. Apparently I'd passed all inspections and the Afghans were eager for me to go. I told them I couldn't wait much longer. Already I'd been away from Pam and Hayne too long and I feared my medical practice was ruined. However, I hated to return home without meeting the legendary Ahmad Shah Massoud. Posters of him were all over Peshawar. He personified their resistance movement. In the refugee camps many male infants were given his name as the parents hoped each child would become the Jesse James-Ronald Reagan-Rambo combination of this legendary leader.

Afghans gathering at the safe house spoke of Massoud in reverential tones, and I was very proud they had selected me to meet him. I suspected they were also anxious to thumb their noses at the Soviets by being able to take an American into the Panjshir Valley and bring him out without being detected.

One chieftain suggested we visit Herat in western Afghanistan to validate reports that a large number of Cuban troops in Russian uniforms were fighting in that area. Herat was Nasir's hometown, so he wanted to return there, but I was sure the trip to the Panjshir Valley would be all we could handle. While discussions continued, I returned to the bazaar and wandered around sopping up local culture and enjoying being regarded as an Afghan. I bought some Afghan brocaded items as gifts for Pam and Hayne, then returned to our home base just in time to be invited to revisit the Gailani family. They were such gracious hosts that I always welcomed the opportunity, only this time I was to be embarrassed by Dr. Daoud.

Mr. Gailani's household was very modern by Afghan standards in that female relatives were allowed to sit with us and listen to our conversations. The ladies always sat very quietly since they spoke no English. Dr. Daoud wanted me to assess their medical conditions and prescribe medications, but there was no way I could determine any of their problems without a history and performing a physical examination was out of the question. He kept insisting and I tried to handle the situation as diplomatically as I could without anyone realizing how upset I was becoming.

Fortunately there was no major *gaffe*, and after we returned to the safe house I let Daoud know in no uncertain terms how I felt. Eventually we settled the disagreement amicably. By the next morning I had cooled down and spent the early hours before dawn assessing my general condition for the ordeal to come.

Since I had not been jogging since leaving home, my stamina was probably a little less than I would have liked, but my intestinal tract seemed to be quiet and my big toes showed no evidence of infection. The hemorrhage under the nails had drained, and I was able to hold the loosened nails in place with adhesive tape. I had adjusted my hiking boots and socks to avoid the trauma to my feet which had occurred while I was in Paktia.

I had developed a rather large boil on my rear end, though. With the aid of a mirror and needle I worked on this for a while, then spent the remainder of the morning waiting for a decision about our trip.

Definite plans had been made for Jane and Diane to leave for Paktia in about four days, but the Afghans had become very concerned about the increasingly bizarre behavior of Dr. Snyder. They diplomatically suggested that he remain in Peshawar and teach at the school for Afghan medics, fearing his total mental and physical collapse if he went "inside." He seemed happy with this decision and spent most of the day off to himself practicing on his harmonica.

My spirits were buoyed by a visit from a Kabul internist/cardiologist who had escaped to Peshawar. At last I was able to discuss clinical medicine. I really enjoyed spending a couple of hours with him comparing medical experiences. Since we were scheduled to dine with Governor Kasem at his home that evening, I skipped the usual meal and passed the afternoon reading my Afghan history book but found the stories of constantly warring tribes tedious.

Supper at the governor's house was delicious. Unfortunately I'd developed ominous stomach cramps and only nibbled. We talked until well past midnight about our plans and the war situation in general. I'd hoped to sleep late but woke early with nothing to do. To relieve the boredom, Nasir and I went to the bazaar and wandered through the mob. I didn't find anything I wanted to buy and decided to save most of my money to obtain presents for Massoud. Back at our place, there was still no word on the trip. The only real change seemed to be an increase in the fly population.

As I was eating or drinking tea, I often pondered if the flies covering the food and glasses had just returned from a trip to our open sewer. Jane and Diane had developed the "Peshawar purge," so Quadrat Nasraty and I smuggled some beer into their room in hopes of improving their moods and fluid balance. Later they reported the beer helped on both accounts.

Thursday, April 5, began as a usual at our sanctuary with no toilet paper, a cold shower and hot tea. The tedium was soon relieved by the arrival of a young turbaned snake charmer who produced wicker baskets full of writhing hissing reptiles. After we paid his modest fee, he reached casually into the baskets and draped fistfuls of snakes all over his head and shoulders until he looked like a dark-skinned male medusa. He danced about, dripping snakes and playing weird tunes on a hollow reed. For a few more rupees he offered to show us the secret of his "magic" stone, which he claimed would extract venom from a snake bite. This sounded interesting!

He aggravated one of the snakes until it bit him on the finger, then squeezed some blood from the two fang marks and rubbed the area with his small "magic" stone. He was careful to keep the stone concealed, but I could see it was about the size of a half-dollar, smooth, with a shallow depression on one side, resembling a "worry" stone. After a little more rubbing, a large drop of straw colored fluid appeared on his finger between the fang marks and he proudly proclaimed that his stone had sucked out all this poison. His sleight of hand was truly impressive and his performance well worth the money. I invited him to come back the following day and bring some cobras.

About dusk a German girl and her boyfriend arrived for dinner. An old friend of Nasir's, she had defected from East Germany while studying languages in Kabul. Her linguistic ability was most impressive. She spoke fluent Pashto, Persian, English, and German, and it was a pleasure talking with this polite and intelligent young lady. In contrast, her boyfriend was a jerk.

He arrogantly rambled on at length about how superior German products were, how American goods were worthless, then proceeded to tell me in great detail all that was wonderful about East Germany and what was wrong with America. I needed to be diplomatic with the Afghans but not with this obnoxious punk. As he informed me that Americans were putting all of their known criminals in uniform and sending them to be stationed in Germany, I leaned close so the Afghans couldn't hear us and whispered, "Young man, everything you have said so far is crap! America whipped Germany's ass in World War II, can easily do it again, and if you don't shut up, this old American is going to whip *your* ass, *Verstehen sie?*'

He glared at me but said no more and pouted for the rest of their visit. My anger seemed to improve my mood, and my disposition was even more improved by learning we should have definite word about our trip the following morning. Soon after we received this cheerful news, the Germans left and we hit the sack.

Dawn arrived heralded by rumbling thunder followed by torrential rain. Nevertheless our snake charmer returned with baskets full of snakes of all sizes, including several cobras. Again he charmed us as well as his snakes while we photographed his performance. His fee of 50 rupees was well deserved. I wasn't surprised that he wouldn't repeat the snake bite trick with the cobras!

After thinking about his demonstration of the "magic stone" the previous day, I'd decided he had allowed the drops of his blood to clot on the stone, then milked off the serum onto his bitten finger. He swore many oaths that the snake he had used was venomous, but of course this wasn't true.

The word arrived: The trip was on!

After the usual multilingual hassle on the telephone, I finally got through to Pam and learned that everything was going well at home. The Afghans clustered around the phone, smiling and nodding as I talked. Our conversation was far from private while I convinced Pam the trip was necessary, and that I would "be careful."

Rain poured in torrents all day long. Poor Jane and Diane were racked with severe diarrhea and vomiting, so I spent much of the day trying to make them more comfortable, primarily by keeping curious Afghans out of their room.

Thunder woke me repeatedly during the night, but thankfully I got enough rest and by dawn was eager for activities to start. It didn't take long. Mass confusion reigned; the door banged as people entered and left, and I couldn't find my clean clothes. Then, after all the chaos, we were informed the trip was delayed again. Since the nurses were still sick their journey was also postponed. Adding to our misery, the toilet stopped, overflowed and flies, flies, flies were everywhere.

Nasir and I fled the confusion and joined the usual mob scene at the bazaar. While in town I wanted to make my plane reservations home and buy presents for Massoud. With Nasir doing the negotiating, I purchased a portable radio and tape player for him, along with vital extra batteries and packed all this in my medical kit. Soon after our return home, Massoud's brother visited to brief us on the details of our mission.

My primary task would be to assess the medical needs of Massoud's forces in terms of equipment and personnel. In addition, I should determine if he would allow US teams to work with his troops and, if so, the risk to these physicians and nurses.

From my interviews with the Afghans in Peshawar, I had already learned something of the ghastly medical conditions in the Panjsher Valley. The intense and prolonged conflict, combined with a lack of any substantial medical care, had raised the mortality rate for abdominal or chest wounds to nearly one hundred percent. Amputation was the only treatment for severe injuries to extremities. Survivors were carried on the backs of other men through the mountains to Peshawar. Obviously any change I could effect in this situation would be an improvement.

I was eager to get started and spent the evening sorting and packing. Beside my basic medical instruments I stashed all the various pills I could accumulate, syringes of morphine and a limited amount of suture material.

At breakfast I learned the trip was again on hold. We were rescheduled to leave the following day, but at this time I'd become frustrated, impatient and homesick. The toilet was plugged, flies seemed to be multiplying geometrically, and the uncertainty was getting on my nerves. My return home would be much later than planned. Pam was due to have her Caesarean section in only 10 days, and I knew I couldn't possibly get back in time for her delivery.

Diane and Jane were feeling better and left in a convoy for the border. Harvey was teaching at the school for Afghan medics, so Nasir, Colonel Osmani and I went shopping for carpet. Since the Colonel had bought and sold carpets in past years, I gladly left the haggling to him and wandered about the shops until the deal was done. He finally settled on one of excellent quality and a reasonable price. The Colonel explained that the beauty of these carpets was enhanced with wear, so the manufacturers would leave newly woven carpets on highways for trucks to run over and season the threads, making the colors more vivid. The carpet he selected for me was beautiful. I hoped Pam would accept it as a peace offering when I got home.

After lunch at Green's Hotel in beautiful downtown Peshawar, we returned home and I spent the rest of the afternoon writing a long letter to Pam and swatting flies.     Harvey came back from his teaching duties, and we walked part-way to town and were caught in a down-pour on our return. When I changed my wet clothes, I found the skin between my toes had rotted, and an infection had developed under both of my big toenails. I worked on these problems for a while, retaped the nails, then went to sleep listening to the gentle patter of rain.

About 11:00 p.m. I was awakened for an emergency house call and rushed through the city to Mr. Gailani's house. His nephew was severely ill with pneumonia. Fortunately I had some antibiotics on hand and left these with him, as well as some medication for his discomfort. We returned to the safe house well after midnight, but I lay wide-awake, tortured with worry about the family and my practice. I'd never been away from the office for more than four or five days at a time and wondered how many of my patients would remain loyal to me, or if I would have any business left when I returned. But most important of all, I needed to be with Pam.

# CHAPTER 8

Shortly before noon an ancient rusted Toyota sedan arrived with the driver and two silent mujahideen armed with Kalashnikovs, pistols and wicked looking curved knives. Conversation was minimal as Nasir, Col. Osmani and I began loading our bags. The jaunty optimism evident before the last trip was painfully absent, and everyone seemed to dread our departure. I knew my Afghan friends were determined to get me in and out of Panjshir Valley safely, but I also sensed they were somewhat uneasy about their chances of success. One by one we walked under the Koran to invoke Allah's blessing for our trip, and Khalifa, our cook, threw a pan of water on the road, a custom that hopefully would ensure our safe return. Those who would be left behind were crying. They hugged us over and over, obviously worried they would never see us again.

As I walked to the car, I was suddenly overcome with a foreboding of doom, but it was far too late to back out. Since I needed to be concealed as much as possible, I was squeezed between two Afghan bodyguards in the back of our old car. There was no room behind the seat, so I stuffed my *patoo* under me and straddled the hump. Although I moved from one cheek to the other every few miles, the boil on my rear end was tenderized as we traveled northeast to the town of Shab-Gadr, our first Pakistani checkpoint.

As we approached the guards, Nasir warned me again to stay in the car. My brown contact lenses, dyed hair and beard, plus the turban and pajama-like *kameez* had fooled other guards earlier, but now we were close to the Afghan border and security was much tighter.

Frowning uniformed men waved us to a halt and cocked their Kalashnikov rifles, snatched the doors open and ordered us out. I stayed in the back seat and pretended to be adjusting my camera while Nasir and the three Afghans were pulled from their seats, loudly protesting the staccato demands of the guards.

A curious crowd gathered at the sight of my companions being pushed and shoved by the screaming guards. Nasir pulled a roll of bills from his kameez to begin negotiations for the usual bribes, but the money was slapped from his hands. I knew then we were in big trouble.

A couple of brisk pokes from a Kalashnikov hastened my exit from the car, and we were herded into a battered truck for a trip to the local court. I tried to act as if I were a haughty, offended Afghan, but I was acutely aware of a river of sweat staining my clothes and hoped no one would guess or smell my fear.

It was apparent the guards had been tipped off. They knew we were coming and, in contrast to all our previous experiences, refused Nasir's bribe. Obviously they had been ordered to place us under arrest.

The courtroom was alive with officials and curious villagers. Nasir had told me to pretend I did not understand English and to answer in German, hoping I could pass as a German journalist. Repeatedly I was asked, "Who are you, Where are you from?" I always responded, *"Nicht verstehe."* The presiding official became more and more exasperated and the men with weapons more threatening.

Nasir whispered in my ear, "They've got us. They know who we are."

So the next time I was asked, "Where are you from?" I yelled "Texas, USA!" There was a short murmur from the onlookers, who then began pointing at me, saying, "Texas, Texas."

The guards hustled us to a truck, and we were taken to an office of the local judge, a very polite Pakistani gentleman in his 40s with a clipped mustache and obvious military bearing. He spoke perfect English with barely a trace of British accent.

"Your honor," I began, "would you please give me the opportunity of explaining who I am and what we are doing here?"

"Of course, I would be very interested in hearing your story. Would you care for tea?"

Naturally I immediately accepted his kind offer. Maybe I wasn't going to jail in Pakistan after all. The judge motioned to one of the scowling guards who returned promptly with steaming tea, glasses and candy. I waited until all had been served and my pulse had slowed, then began my plea.

First, I stated I had no wish to upset his community, and apologized for the disturbance. I was an American doctor who wanted only to pass through his area to reach Afghanistan, when I hoped to provide badly needed medical care to the suffering people of that war-torn country. I admitted what we were doing was a little outside the law (to put it mildly) but asked his forbearance and permission to continue.

When I'd finished my spiel, he sipped his tea, thought a moment and answered: "Doctor, I am in great sympathy with what you are trying to accomplish and I applaud your motives. However, I am a man of law, and what you are doing is clearly illegal. Therefore, as a judge, I cannot countenance or approve an illegal act. I am sure you understand. Also, you see, you have chosen to pass through my district and I have officially seen you here. If something unfortunate should happen to you while you are in Afghanistan, as would seem very likely, there would be an investigation and you would be traced back to this checkpoint. For these reasons I cannot let you pass, but I will impose no fine or sentence if you and your party agree to turn around and cease your illegal efforts to enter Afghanistan."

What could I do but agree? After thanking him profusely for his hospitality we left his office and were carried back in their truck to our battered sedan, all the time trying to ignore the loud threats and ridicule from the crowd. No one spoke as we headed back toward Peshawar, depressed that our plans had failed.

A couple of miles down the road, I startled everyone by suddenly erupting, "Damn it, Nasir, I didn't come this far and invest this much time to be turned back now. I know what I promised the judge, but we've made all these plans. There must be some other way to get into Afghanistan besides going through his village. I would rather go to *jail* than return to Peshawar now and go home."

Nasir looked shocked for a moment, then suddenly began a rapid-fire conversation with our driver. The others joined in while I sat mutely waiting for the results of this intense *jirgah*, the Afghans' beloved version of verbal fisticuffs. When we reached a crossroad, Nasir pointed to the left fork and spoke to the driver. He gunned our little car down the new road as everyone cheered, and I knew we were beginning another run for the border.

The dust and heat of the first leg of our journey faded as we headed north through the most enchanting valley I'd seen in this part of the world. Large orchards were bordered by well-tended fields of lush green vegetables and swaying wheat. Storybook like villages of castles and fortified towers perched atop each hill. Yellow, red and white flowers carpeted the valleys. We had entered Pashtonistan, land of the fearless fighters. These scenes of peaceful beauty seemed to contradict their legendary violent reputation.

Spiraling down into a sheltered valley, we followed a winding dusty road beside a narrow gauge railroad which paralleled the river. In the distance I noticed a crossing blocked by a wooden barricade and armed guards. We slowed and waited for a caravan of large trucks to go by us, then our driver whipped the Toyota in between two of them in a maneuver so abrupt I ducked my head and waited for the crash. Sandwiched between the two massive vehicles, we roared through the checkpoint before the guards realized we were there. They yelled at us to come back but for some unknown reason didn't shoot. Before they could set up a chase, we were long gone from the village of Bokhara.

There were no more checkpoints between us and the border, so we rested, munching on oranges and bananas at the next picturesque village. Everyone was hugging and congratulating each other about our newfound success. We transferred from the car to a small pickup of uncertain make and vintage and headed closer to the Afghan border, blinded now by sheets of rain. Our driver, obviously lost, had to backtrack several times in the dark before we reached the small village of Timor-Gara and on past this outpost to a small farm. The downpour had become even more intense. We huddled around a smoky fire in the barn to cook a Spartan meal of cabbage and tea. The cabbage was gritty, but I ate my fill, not knowing when I would have another meal.

It was too dark to write in my journal, so I went out on the porch to operate my small transcriber and record the day's events. Something was wrong with the machine. I would speak a few sentences, reverse the tape and try again. While I was working on it, I heard the heart-stopping clicks of Kalashnikovs being cocked and stared into the barrels of four guns held by very hostile-looking strangers. Obviously they thought I was radioing information to the enemy and were set to silence me *pronto*. I yelled frantically for Nasir, but an eternity seemed to pass before he appeared and saved me. In the future, I decided it would be prudent to write in my journal regardless of the difficulty and keep the recorder buried in the bottom of my pack.

All the stresses of this day had exhausted me, and after one pit stop by flashlight in the pouring rain I slept soundly until awakened at dawn for the final leg of our journey.

The morning weather was as foul as everyone's humor. Last night we'd taken a wrong road so everyone was grumbling when we piled into the pickup to back-track. I felt so grungy I wanted to sit in the back of the truck and air out a little, but Nasir insisted that I stay in the cab in case we made another wrong turn and ran into more border guards.

Before we entered the village of Anat Bazaar, a cold rain drenched the men in the back, although they tried to cover themselves with a wrinkled plastic sheet. The old truck leaked in front almost as badly, and everyone was frozen and soaked by the time we reached a tea house. The usual long *jirgah* began while I daydreamed and waited for someone to fill me in on the results of the conversation. Finally Nasir told me they were discussing the best route to the border and again emphasized that I should try to keep out of sight as much as possible.

Once we entered Afghanistan, our problems would multiply. No doubt the Soviets would try to kill or capture us, and many of the hill tribesmen were equally hostile to strangers. Although most villages were vehemently anti-Soviet, the people were desperate and might turn us over to the enemy in order to avoid reprisals to their village or to obtain food. As much as possible I'd try to continue my disguise as a German journalist. From now on we would not be carrying weapons, since some of the tribesmen would murder us to get them. I was also warned that in the poorer areas they might kill us for our boots. At the first opportunity my boots would join the transcriber in my pack, and I would put on my old jogging shoes.

During our discussion I made a comment I would regret many times in the future. I told Nasir I wished to travel as an Afghan this trip. I wanted no special considerations and wanted to be one of them. I was to eat what they ate, sleep where they slept and learn what it was like to be an Afghan during wartime. Only ignorance could foster such bravado. Had I known what pain and misery lay in the path of an Afghan warrior, such foolish words would have never crossed my lips.

The storm finally slackened and we roared away in the old unmuffled truck. Afghan drivers have only two speeds: stop and wide open. While we raced through the countryside past many rustic cemeteries, I was depressed to note the large number of tiny graves. These gave mute testimony to the high infant mortality rate—at least eighty percent even in the relative safety of Pakistan.

Aside from the innumerable graveyards, the countryside was beautiful. Large fields of grain, amazing irrigation systems and huge checkerboard fields of red and white opium poppies speckled the hilly terrain. We left the main highway and followed a primitive road through valleys surrounding forbidding fortress-like houses and looming stone forts which served as outposts for the Pakistani militia. There were no power lines, TV antennas or other signs of modern civilization to be seen. This was truly the northwest frontier of British colonial days. I'd entered the land of my boyhood fantasies.

Arriving at the base of a mountain, our Afghan driver gunned the old truck for all it was worth, and we reeled up the muddy winding road, sliding sideways with wheels spinning. Many times I thought our trip would end on this ascent and kept one hand on the door handle ready to jump. We whipped around a curve sideways in a power slide, then stopped just short of a gigantic rock fall. From now until we returned to Pakistan we would walk. In the drizzling rain we continued our ascent on foot and I discovered another quaint Afghan custom—they never follow a road. It seems to be a mark of personal honor to walk straight up the side of a mountain, ignoring the easier path. I followed them as best I could, stopping frequently to catch my breath. At the stroke of noon we reached the summit which towered high above an opaque sheet of gray clouds. Without a pause the Afghans and I once again crossed into the ravaged country of Afghanistan.

We descended through the cloud layer and immediately were pelted by a cold steady rain. The downhill slope was almost as difficult as the ascent, so steep that herds of goats on the mountainside could feed on leaves in the treetops. We clumped down a dizzying trail for almost an hour, halting for lunch at a small roadside teahouse beside a tumbling waterfall. By the time we'd finished our tea, the frigid drizzle had stopped and we walked into a rocky valley surrounded by wheat fields, irrigation canals and miles and miles of waving red and white opium poppies.

Always there was another ascent. We followed a streambed uphill for three hours, and then loped down into another valley. All along the trail rocks were splattered with blood. I never discovered the source of this blood, whether it was from an animal or wounded soldier. Late in the evening we stopped at a sturdy, hillside mosque consisting of a large, open room covered by massive hand-carved beams. A small stream ran through the mosque, allowing my companions to perform their ablutions in relative comfort before evening prayer.

The sound of Soviet artillery had increased all day but ceased at dark, allowing us to enjoy a supper of tea, a few dates and chicken broth. I fell asleep long before anyone else. The night was punctuated by the usual traffic of armed tribesmen, inevitably accompanied by loud greetings and conversation.

Sleep was also interrupted by a new and unpleasant sensation. Small animals were crawling over me, and I knew lice were hitchhiking in my sleeping bag and on my body. I couldn't sleep and lay awake scratching, passing the time by mentally reviewing my companions; these men who would determine the success of our mission and my chances of living through this foray.

Our group was led by a large tough old Afghan known only as *"Baba,"* which means old man, but he certainly didn't act old when climbing mountains, fording streams or leading us along the trail. His belongings were stuffed in his *patoo*, which he carried over his shoulder Santa Claus style. Perpetually in a hurry, he constantly prodded me to go faster. Several times a day I fumed at his impatience and his killing pace, but I never stopped admiring his stamina. His only words to me were *"Beelah, beelah"* (Hurry, hurry)—so often that I began to think my name was *"Beelah."*

Akbar, a tiny elf-like creature in his 20s, wore a pillbox hat. His *patoo* was tied around his neck like a cape. He disappeared for hours; then as we struggled up an exhausting climb, I'd spy him sitting on a rock high above like a leprechaun waiting for us to catch up. While we descended a precipitous slope grabbing for branches to slow our fall, he'd run head-long down the hill at such a pace his body was almost perpendicular to the slope and his *patoo* streamed out behind him. I called him "Batman" for the rest of the trip.

Noor was a very dark-skinned Afghan, who looked to be in his early 40s and smoked cigarettes incessantly. Although he tired a little earlier than the others, he was still able to climb and forge along the passes much better than I. His friendly smile was our only means of communication.

Nasir always stayed far ahead of the rest of us, going up and down canyons on his own, seeking out the trail, and constantly demonstrating he was the hardiest of the group. I soon learned not to follow him as he often found dead ends and frequently became lost. He was, however, my only source of information. No one else spoke a word of English. When I chose not to follow him, I never knew what was going on and had to stumble along blindly, trusting the man in front of me.

Colonel Osmani, a strong man in his mid-40s, was my constant friend and support. He was always ready to help me up the slopes, waited while I forded streams and gave me a rapid refresher course in German, our only mutual language. With his help and patience, it was amazing how much German I recalled from college days, though my pronunciation was a never-ending source of amusement to him. Many times in the coming weeks I would owe him my life. He was the treasurer of our group and carried money for bribes, food and porters in a money belt I had given him.

Naim, one of Massoud's lieutenants, was a large husky Afghan in his mid-20s built like a football lineman. He wore captured Russian boots and a broad leather belt with his *kameez*, as well as a distinctive black and white checked turban. His strength was impressive, which he demonstrated by easily lifting me over his head. This stunt would become less difficult for him as the trip progressed and I melted away on our poor diet.

During a tea break, Nasir related a typical story about Naim. When 18 years old, he wanted to join the *mujahideen* but didn't have a rifle. Equipment was so scarce in those days that in order to join the fighters, each man had to furnish his own weapon. One night Naim was hiding with some friends on a mountainside overlooking a village that had been captured by the Soviets. He borrowed an old rifle, went down into the village square, and as Nasir said, "Just like your John Wayne," challenged the Russians to come out and fight.

Five Soviet soldiers armed with Kalashnikovs emerged shooting. Ignoring their withering fire, Naim methodically killed the lot, picked up their weapons and returned to the camp. After this episode he was promptly accepted into Massoud's forces and began his legendary career.

Jawad, of undetermined age, was a very mysterious person with the distinctive oriental features of a Central Asian. He seldom spoke to me or any of the others, ate alone and always unrolled his *patoo* far away from us for his private prayers. For long periods he would silently stare at me, and I had the uneasy feeling he would cheerfully slit my throat with the slightest provocation. I avoided this man as much as possible.

Young men in their early 20s were hired as porters, usually staying with us for five or ten miles until we reached the next village and new porters were found. They knew the local trails, were extremely tough and usually walked far ahead of the rest of us.

# CHAPTER 9

While the loud morning prayer call echoed through the mosque, I awakened on the cool morning of April 10 and began packing. Every day at this time I wondered how many times I would experience total exhaustion before dark.

Our prayers were soon drowned out by the booming of nearby artillery, and the din increased as we walked down the trail. I ran ahead to take some pictures of our departure but was sharply called back by Nasir and told to stay back in the line of our single file. My heart skipped a beat when I was informed of the fact that we were walking through our first mine field! After about five hours cautiously moving downhill through the colorful but deadly poppy fields, we paused for sweet tea and cookies that could have been used for paving stones.

A crumbling rock wall surrounded a small cemetery at the edge of the field, black pennants on tall poles marking the graves of fallen *mujahideen*. From some long-forgotten college course I recalled the lines of John McCrae:

*"We are the Dead, short days ago we lived, felt dawn, saw sunset glow, loved and were loved, and now we lie in Flanders Fields."*

Only a slight change of the last line to "Afghan fields" made the epitaph appropriate and equally affecting.

Just when we started walking again, mortar shells erupted on the trail behind and in front of us. Should we follow the trail which was obviously zeroed in on by the Soviet mortars, or flee through the heavily mined fields? I left this decision to the others but made sure I stayed in line as instructed.

Then the jets came. As each MIG screamed overhead we hid under the rock walls of the fields or in the ditches and dashed along the trail again when they disappeared. Roaring jets and the rumble of artillery accompanied our jerky progress all morning. No bombs were dropped, and fortunately there was little strafing. But it was not a particularly enjoyable way to spend a morning hike.

Because our progress was delayed by the hostile activity, two men were sent ahead to locate a ferry. We moved as rapidly as possible in small groups through the terraced fields and reached the river by mid-morning.

Naim, a young porter, and "Batman" in the Poppy Fields.

Snow was melting in the mountains causing the usually placid Kunar River to become a raging torrent at least 200 yards wide. One by one we clambered down the side of a muddy cliff to the ferry, a skeletal arrangement of poles lashed together over inflated cowhides. There was no time to test our raft's stability, and we cast off immediately. Two Afghans rowed desperately, while another constantly blew air into a leg of the cowhide to keep it inflated. The rest of us tried to hang on as we slanted through the waves across the churning current. Before we reached mid-stream, the noise of our progress was drowned by the ominous, roaring pulsations of approaching helicopters. This time I was sure I'd never see home again. We were defenseless. There was nothing to do but keep going.

The helicopters passed just above our heads, almost deafening us. Unbelievably, the Soviets showed no interest, and we reached the far shore as they disappeared in the distance. Nasir shouted at me to hurry up the rocky bank into the meager shelter of some trees. I needed no prompting and had clawed my way up the cliff and into a level area when he suddenly yelled for me to stop and be still. I thought the helicopters were returning but Nasir screamed that I was standing in a minefield. I glanced nervously around and saw tiny bits of green plastic scattered everywhere—my first introduction to "butterfly bombs."

The Soviets had dumped thousands of these palm-sized explosive plastic devices from their planes and helicopters. They were strewn everywhere, but particularly in the grain fields tended by women and small children. If a child stepped on a butterfly bomb, or picked it up thinking it was a toy, there was just enough explosive to blow off a hand or foot. They were cunningly designed to maim, rather than kill, for if the hapless child survived his injury, the family would have to take him to Pakistan for medical care, and another family would be lost to the resistance forces. These fiends were targeting their war directly on women and children.

Soaked in nervous sweat, I tiptoed slowly through the bits of plastic and unexploded mines as if walking on eggshells, while the others waited patiently by the riverbank. There was nothing they could do until I finally cleared the field and made my way along the riverbank to join them. Nasir didn't need to caution me again to keep in line while we gingerly crossed abandoned roadbeds and scaled nearby hills.

We were dangerously exposed. Trees were scarce and barely larger

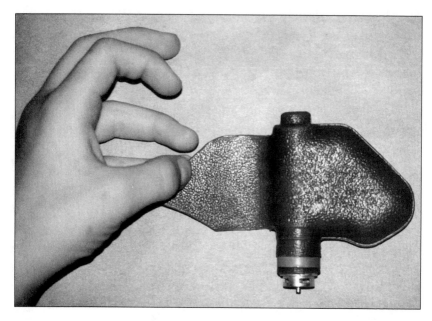

"Butterfly Bomb"

than shrubs. We could still hear the helicopters and jets behind the next ridge. When their noise subsided, we walked at a more leisurely pace, always on the alert. Scattered pieces of plastic were everywhere. I picked up a pocketful of fragments in hopes of reconstructing a bomb to document this monstrous atrocity.

When we paused for tea and some cheese under a huge sycamore tree, I arranged some of the parts in what I thought would resemble an unexploded bomb and took a picture. Later this proved unnecessary as I was given several intact bombs emptied of explosive and detonators. The empty casings were sometimes used by the resourceful Afghans as snuffboxes.

After a short brisk walk, we paused to drink from a small spring at the base of a looming mountain, and Colonel Osmani asked me to keep his watch while he washed up for prayer. Then we commenced hand-over-hand climbing almost straight up. Many times I didn't think I would make it and lay gasping, but Baba would prod me to climb again. Part way up I found a small stick to use as a staff and carried it for the rest of my journey. Although several inches were worn from the tip by the time our trek was completed, I brought it home as a reminder of those days.

We climbed higher. I ate snow to relieve my thirst and chewed handfuls of violet flowers to reduce my nausea. In spite of stops every five minutes and water at the multiple gushing springs, I was exhausted long before we reached the summit. From the top of this mountain it seemed we could see forever. The sun setting over snow-capped peaks was reflected in a silver stream winding through the verdant valley far below—a wonderland of well-tended orchards, green fields of swaying wheat and patchwork squares of opium poppies. When my eyes feasted on this beautiful scene, I considered how this idyllic view illustrated one of the occult horrors of this terrible war.

In the valley, Afghans struggled to plant enough wheat to sustain their starving families and cultivated poppies for the heroin market. Earlier, as we walked through the poppy fields, Nasir and I had discussed this flourishing trade. I learned some of the opium base was carried into Pakistan to be sold or traded for arms and equipment, but a large portion was made available to Soviet troops in an attempt to get them addicted. This plan had been extremely successful, not so much in the front-line Soviet troops who were doing the fighting, but with the rear echelons, motor pools and support troops. Heroin was traded to them for equipment or money, and there was an unceasing demand for the drug.

Nasir showed me a leaflet prepared by the Afghans and distributed to the Soviet soldiers. I understood none of the Russian printed on the pamphlet, but it was interpreted as, "Why don't you leave our homeland? We only want our freedom. Leave us to our mountains and our families and there will be peace."

In my opinion, selling heroin would prove to be more effective in the quest for peace than appealing to the mercy of the Soviets, for thus far I had seen no evidence of compassion on either side. As a physician and as an American, I was in vigorous opposition to the illicit drug trade, but I could understand the desperation of these people using any means available to survive.

While I sat quietly pondering this dilemma, Nasir took me aside and quietly told me to stop giving the "thumbs up" sign when we reached a summit or did something good. To an Afghan, he explained kindly, this gesture was the same as the obscene extended middle-finger sign of Americans. I had made another cultural miscue.

Our break was over. I wobbled on rubbery legs down the steep grade and arrived at a small hovel. It was just before dark. I was too tired to eat, but the others enjoyed a very noisy meal, accompanied by their customary loud talking and incessant coming and going through a painfully squeaking door. I'll never forget the sound of my Afghan companions eating in the dark, cracking the bones of chicken and sucking out the marrow.

While they were having their evening *jirgah*, I undressed in my sleeping bag and donned an old Carolina sweatshirt as pajamas. Being partially clean made my rest more pleasant in spite of the tiny critters crawling all over me. I'd survived another day and the hardest climb thus far. But I couldn't find Colonel Osmani's watch. I packed and unpacked my gear, trying in my fractured German to have him understand my distress. He was very gracious, but I knew his watch was very precious to him. At last Nasir found the watch tangled in his prayer blanket. How it got there I don't know, but finding it allowed me to sleep.

We were up and packing before 5:00 a.m. While I waited for tea to boil, I wandered around the area a bit. Much to my surprise I met an old Afghan wearing a University of Texas tee-shirt under his jacket. Despite my attempts at sign language I could never learn where he had found the shirt. But at least for me, it was a glimpse of home.

"Baba"

I welcomed the downhill grade at the start of our walk, but the trail was covered with loose pebbles and I was constantly stumbling and grabbing trees to break my fall. As a result I suffered a considerable loss of skin from my hands and elbows. Day by day I could tell I was growing weaker. By the time we reached the valley and began ascending the next mountain I was as exhausted at mid-morning as I'd been the afternoon of the previous day. Canned cheese, Vienna sausage and hot tea only partially revived me. By 8:30 a.m. I was beginning to see spots before my eyes and was dreadfully thirsty but avoided drinking the water in the few hillside villages we passed. Much to my relief, others in our group seemed almost as tired as I, and our pace slowed.

After frequent pauses we reached the summit just before noon and hid in some scrub bushes until the routine Soviet reconnaissance planes had passed. By this time I was beginning to welcome the Soviet Air Force since their flights forced us to stop, and I could enjoy a respite.

By early afternoon everyone in the group seemed worn out—except Baba. Another old Afghan came up from behind and passed us at a rapid pace, not even breathing hard. He'd walked in a day the distance we'd covered in the previous two. This was even more shameful since I had to be pushed and pulled up at least the last half mile to the summit. I knew I was slowing us down but couldn't help it. I was moving as fast as I could. At each village I even hoped that we would find a horse. No such luck.

On one of the climbs, Naim wrapped his turban tightly around my middle like a girdle and indicated this would help my breathing. He also made me swallow a handful of vitamin C tablets. Medically I didn't think much of his treatment, but any help was welcome, even the effect of a placebo. I tried to get my mind on other things to diminish the fatigue of the climb. All I could think of was Pam's Cesarean section due in one week and how much I wanted to be home.

At the peak we rested half an hour, then tumbled down an almost vertical incline without a visible trail. As usual, Batman raced down, never falling, with his *patoo* streaming out behind him. I slid along on my bottom till this became too painful, then semi-jogged down, digging my heels in the dirt and rocks and grabbing at tree limbs to slow my speed. Sometimes I just fell on the ground to stop. About halfway we found a spring filling a mossy stagnant water trough. Splashing water all over my face and hair partially revived me. I drank my fill in spite of the bugs and goat pellets. Lunch was only tepid water and cold goat meat before we continued to descend the grade into a hillside village that overlooked the river far below. All of the young men of the group, including the porters, appeared extremely tired; the older men acted as if they were on a holiday jaunt.

We found a decent trail crisscrossing the remainder of the slope, but of course we didn't stay on it and blazed a difficult and rocky path across many terraced fields into the valley. There we discovered what could pass as a road zig-zagging along the valley, pot-holed with bomb craters. We passed wrecked and burned tanks, armored personnel carriers and trucks destroyed in previous battles. The mud-daubed hamlets were lifeless and abandoned. Sprawling graveyards peppered with black pennant flags provided silent evidence of the terrible events that had transpired here.

During a short break I learned the reason we'd climbed the two previous mountain ranges. A large Soviet outpost controlled the river valley where we now camped. We would have had to pass by this outpost had we taken the easy route. By the time we stopped for the night in a small settlement, we'd walked at least twelve hours. I fell asleep worrying how much longer I could keep up the pace.

Before 5:00 a.m. everyone was up and about, and the usual chatter started in the darkness. "When one Afghan is awake, the whole world awakens."

I sat under a sheltering leafy tree and wrote in my journal while bags were weighed and new porters hired. Colonel Osmani negotiated the use of several tiny donkeys, and we loaded a portion of our gear on these most unwilling beasts. I was told to climb on one so small I was forced to hold my feet up to keep them from dragging the ground. Of course there was no bridle or saddle. The diminutive animal sagged, unable to bear my weight and began feeble attempts to dump me in the river. I don't know which of us felt sorrier for the other. I finally refused to ride the poor animal, which caused a hassle. Nasir wasn't around to translate my refusal. When he did arrive, there was another brief (for the Afghans) *jirgah*, and the donkeys were sent back to the village. We and the porters were forced to share the baggage.

Despite a disastrous beginning, the morning walk was splendid. We followed a fairly wide road that wound up and down rolling hills through lush irrigated fields and passed village after village that appeared relatively undamaged by the war. We saw only a few bombed-out buildings, compared to the total destruction of all the settlements we'd seen on yesterday's trail.

Pausing under a small grove of trees beside an aqueduct, I experienced the eerie sensation that we had suddenly moved back in time. No wrecked vehicles or vehicles of any sort were visible, just primitive plows pulled by oxen. There was nothing to suggest modern life. While the others rested, I walked by an aqueduct built of small stones that guided a stream of icy water into a grain mill about the size of a small outhouse. Inside, roaring water gushed over a handmade wooden wheel which engaged spokes and gears which turned the grinding stone. I sat mesmerized by the primitive machinery, and was transported back to the 18th century.

Outside I submitted to a sudden impulse and lay down in the tiny stream. The water was shockingly cold, but I forced myself to lie still while my companions laughed and pointed at my crazy behavior. When I finally got up, shivering and shaking, I felt at least a little cleaner and hoped the frigid water had drowned most of my body lice. The sun was warm, so I was dry and comfortable within an hour.

We walked until noon, then entered a dense grove of large trees surrounding a wide aqueduct. Again I felt as if I'd entered another world. The Pech Valley we had just passed through had been captivating. This area was absolutely spectacular. I stopped and stared, knowing how Dorothy must have felt when she left her black and white Kansas farm to enter the Technicolor Land of Oz.

The aqueduct entered a small clearing, and the water flowed over a large wheel which creakingly powered another flour mill. Soft green grass carpeted the ground and the sweet smell of mint flavored the air. Cool sparkling water continued its guided course from the flour mill to flow gently under the porch of a rustic mosque built of huge stones and massive, carved wooden beams. Towering trees shaded the entire area.

Pyramids of Kalashnikovs, ammunition belts and grenades were stacked on the porch while bearded *mujahideen* washed up for prayer in the stream flowing underneath the mosque. We were all welcomed with traditional hugs and kisses. Then I sat on a large rock at the edge of the clearing while our group joined the fighters in their prayers, all facing their weapons. It seemed to me as though they were worshipping Allah and guns simultaneously. My own prayers joined with the Muslims' in this primitive cathedral.

After prayers we gathered in the mosque to eat, and I was offered a large bowl of buttermilk that contained a huge lump of rock salt. Since childhood

I've hated buttermilk and politely refused the offer several times. Finally, at their insistence, I took a cautious sip. It was cold, tangy and salty and easily the most delicious drink I have ever tasted. Immediately my life-long aversion ended, and they almost didn't get their bowl back.

I shall never forget the "Buttermilk Mosque" and that evening of communion with my Muslim brothers. While I shared their bread and drank buttermilk from their tin chalice it seemed we had made our commitment to each other.

When the buttermilk had been drunk, our newfound friends shouldered their weapons and marched off in one direction while we went our way following the turbulent river. The joy of the morning was soon rinsed away by a blinding rain. Our packs were soaked, everyone was miserable, and at first no one was talking. But as we slopped along through the mud and downpour, my companions began to chatter, which for some reason developed into a heated argument. I kept looking for Nasir to translate, but he'd forged far ahead. The argument got louder, and I became more disgusted with the whole situation. Cursing at the top of my lungs, my voice drowned out the others as I complained about never treating patients, being wasted as a doctor and wearing myself out for no good reason.

Since no one understood my rantings, Nasir was summoned to find out why I had lost my mind. By the time he arrived I'd shut up, cooled down and was almost laughing at myself.

We squished along in the rain and dark for another hour or so and finally stopped to sleep in a barn packed with wet smelly cows. When I opened my bag, I discovered my liquid soap had spilled over everything. I became semi-hysterical, laughing at my soaked, cold, hungry and now soapy condition. I walked out into the pouring rain to an irrigation ditch, cleaned up the mess and returned to settle down for the night in soaking wet clothes.

The next morning I woke to find I'd made my bed in several large cow patties. At this point I simply shrugged. The continuing rain would wash off this newest pungent mess in no time. We'd skipped supper the night before, and there was no breakfast. Everyone was soaked, cold, shivering and miserable as we silently slogged through a wheat field.

Suddenly a young girl ran screaming from one of the huts. The Afghans' mouths hung open in amazement at this spectacle. Not only was a woman having the audacity to speak directly to them, but was eloquently chewing them out for trampling her wheat. After an excellent tongue-lashing, she returned to her hut and everyone squished on, thoroughly chastened, while I wished I could hug this young lady for her spirit.

We crossed and recrossed the river on several rickety foot bridges, then began to climb. The higher we went, the more the temperature dropped. This new misery was aggravated by our soggy clothes. Soon the rain turned to sleet.

Halfway to the summit we rested in a small lean-to on the side of the mountain and were joined by a traveler who was returning to Peshawar. I wrote a brief message to Harvey asking him to tell Pam I was going to be delayed but not to worry. I doubted the message would ever be delivered, but it made me feel a little better to at least have tried. I was too cold to write in my journal and there was no wood for a fire, so we climbed on through the sleet, then struggled upward through clinging snow all the way to the peak.

Over the top and down the other side through snow, then sleet, then rain, we waded hip-deep across an icy stream and traipsed up and down hills through many small hamlets. Slogging up a steep hill toward a much larger settlement, it quickly became apparent the rain had flushed the town's community toilet. All varieties of feces poured down the trail around our ankles. By then I'd become an expert on various forms of excrement and amused myself by identifying human, goat, cow, dog and poultry droppings. When I looked up, there were beautiful jagged snowcapped peaks at eye level less than a mile or so away, but this was the filthiest community containing the filthiest people I had ever beheld.

The children were gaunt, half-starved and never smiled. They stared silently at me from deep-sunken, glazed, dead eyes. Women and children moved like zombies up the trail carrying huge loads of firewood. As always, I was amazed at their hardiness, but agonized over their miserable conditions.

Filthy but friendly Afghans directed us to a large room on the second floor of their hillside mosque. From the noise and small faces peering in at us, it seemed we had been housed in the local childcare center. An old fuel drum in the center of the room was filled with blazing wood so we huddled close. Colonel Osmani left to bargain for food.

Steam rose from our clothes. As we began to dry out, what a stink! Worse than any locker room. So bad we could almost taste the odor. Somehow the stove vent became plugged and the room filled with smoke. We were forced

The starving, fly-covered children—everywhere.

to lie flat on the floor in order to breathe. If I raised my head even slightly, I began coughing. In desperation, Noor kicked out one of the paper windows, which provided some escape for the smoke, but no one was able to stand or walk without paroxysms of coughing. Naim had developed severe bronchitis, so I located some sulfa and aspirin in my bag and began his treatment. If he became incapacitated, who would pull me up the mountains? Finally the smoke cleared, and we huddled once more around the fire.

Our food arrived, a big meal of tea, bread, goat cheese and *pinto beans*. I ate almost the whole bowl—at last something with salt and some flavor. Afterward I was terribly thirsty, but from the looks of this community I thought it wise to stick to boiled tea and avoid local water.

Nasir returned with more discouraging news. The ascent tomorrow would be the roughest one yet—steep, cold and through deep snow. When I wrote in my journal, I asked Nasir for the name of this village as I wanted to remember it—Kor-dar—as the worst place we had visited.

We flopped on the straw floor and tried to sleep, but it was a rough night because of the smoke and being forced to listen to a crazy old man scream to Allah all night.

When the first glimmer of dawn shot through the smashed window I awoke dreading the pending struggle in such icy cold. I dressed in long underwear and hiking boots, then added my hooded coat and woolen gloves. We began our trek before dawn, but no one complained. All of us were happy to leave Kor-dar as quickly as possible.

We'd had stopped walking early in the afternoon of the previous day, so I hoped extra rest and a reasonably good supper would give me enough stamina for our trek. Nasir was in a foul mood and grumbled all morning about our shabby treatment by our hosts. Nothing seemed to enrage an Afghan more than poor hospitality. The young men hired to carry our packs were increasing their fees, and we'd been terribly over-charged for last night's meal. To top it all off, Nasir had hardly slept at all.

We began a slow but steady climb over rocks and terraces, crossing and recrossing an icy stream. In spite of the cold, I soon became drenched with sweat and was breathing hard, very grateful when we stopped about 8:00 a.m. to rest. I was always ready for the tea and prayer breaks, which gave me a chance to rest before the next ordeal. Only this time there was no tea. We shared some warm goat's milk and a few chunks of gritty bread that tasted like cardboard. The cheese bought in Kor-dar was riddled with goat pellets, and packed so much hair some pieces looked as if they could stand a good shave. I nibbled very cautiously on these exotic morning treats.

The mountain exceeded my worst fears. We struggled in snow up to our hips the entire time. I began to count each step, trying to reach fifty before stopping, but as we rose higher the number became smaller and smaller. The exhaustion I had experienced the day before was nothing to compare with this. First I developed tunnel vision, then I heard roaring in my head as if wind were blowing down from the summit. My chest heaved wildly, and I passed out.

An Afghan rubbing snow in my face and slapping me on the head awakened me. It took at least two hours to flounder up the next mile; most of the time I had to be pushed or pulled. With each step I imagined we'd reached the summit. I'd shoot a baleful glance skyward only to find we had more jagged ridges to surmount. At 2:30 p.m. I finally staggered to the top, nearly three hours later than we'd planned. I could tell the others were disgusted with my snail's pace and were beginning to doubt I could make it over the still higher mountains to come. At that moment I didn't think anything could be worse.

I trudged slowly down the grade, but my companions moved faster and faster, leaving me so far behind I could barely see them through the gathering fog. Apparently they had decided to abandon me in the snow. In spite of my best efforts, I was unable to force my body to speed up and the Afghans disappeared into the mist.

Stumbling along in their tracks as best I could, I fell and slid over fifty yards down the ice-glazed slope and slammed into a boulder. Anything was better than being left behind to die, so I lay on my back, pulled the fatigue jacket up between my legs like a big diaper, lifted my feet in the air, and slid down the hill like a misshaped toboggan. The next half-mile I bounced over boulders the size of basketballs only to crash to a stop against others. Then I would force myself to start again.

My new mountaineering technique allowed me to overtake my companions at the snow line and join them for mid-afternoon tea. My feet, legs and hands were going numb, and I had no doubt my body would be a patchwork of ugly purple bruises.

When we commenced our long descent into the valley I became more concerned about frostbite. I wiggled my toes as much as I could while I walked and counted my steps. Every fifty paces I slapped my hands on my sides, then would blow my breath on my fingers to keep them warm. After eating rank goat cheese for breakfast and not using a toothbrush for several days, it's a wonder my breath didn't rot my fingernails off.

Leaving the snow behind, we jumped from one Volkswagen-sized boulder to another, crossed rivulets of melting snow, then entered a forest of gigantic trees surrounded by sheer cliffs. The terrain brought memories of Santa Helena Canyon on the Texas-Mexico border.

By now I was so exhausted I fell every few yards. Once again the Afghans left me far behind. I tottered my way through the forest and tried to follow their tracks, hoping they would eventually stop and wait for me. I prayed they hadn't turned off to follow a trail I hadn't recognized.

After dark I tripped even more frequently and was constantly afraid of breaking or spraining something. In this harsh environment even a trivial injury could prove fatal without medical care. At the very least it might slow me down enough to be captured by the Soviets.

After suffering through two hours of stumbling alone in the dark, I found my companions huddled in an old roofless shelter, trying to start a fire. They had finally stopped walking when it had become too dark, not out of any concern for me. We had no food, tea or sleeping bags, for the porters had traveled far ahead with our supplies. No one spoke. The entire group was tired, miserable and hostile.

I hung my shoes and socks to dry by the tiny fire while I carefully warmed my numb feet. Surprisingly, I found no areas of frostbite, and although I was almost asphyxiated by the acrid smoke of our little brush fire, the warmth was welcome. I crouched in a corner of the hut and dozed with my head on my knees. All of us slept poorly, shivering from the bitter cold and coughing from the pungent smoke.

When the first rays of sunlight that offered no warmth shot over the ragged peaks to the east we began trudging along the stream, then stopped for a short rest about 6:30 a.m. Not only was I becoming more fatigued with each passing day but more discouraged. The Afghans seemed to be floundering about almost as much as I was, for our "leader" lost his way repeatedly, forcing us to backtrack several times. I took Nasir aside to confide in him that I was getting much weaker and feared I wouldn't be able to make another climb like yesterday's. But I was too proud to have him or Colonel Osmani keep pulling me along. From our brief conversation I knew my condition worried all of them. Their attempt to thumb their noses at the Soviets with an American might end in disaster for all of us.

Just before 7:30 a.m. we arrived at a community of terraced, multistoried adobe-like houses clinging precariously to the steep cliffs. Our porters had spent a comfortable night there and cheerfully awaited our arrival and another trek.

Warm tea revived me somewhat, and I found a package of freeze-dried beef stroganoff in the bottom of one of the bags. It was cold and somewhat mushy, but at least it was food, the first I'd eaten since the Vienna sausage and beans of two days ago.

The commander of this village (Bozorq-Khel) high in the Teteen Valley was a former student of Colonel Osmani, and they enjoyed a hearty reunion. Commander Qasem proudly demonstrated his portable radio and flashlight, both very significant status symbols in any remote Afghan village. With obvious pride, he then showed me the village privy. It was well used and very pungent, but certainly an improvement over the unchanneled sewage of Kor-dar. Next, Qasem generously provided a pan of warm water and a room for a bath of sorts. I sponged off as best I could and was able to wash my hair, drowning most of the crawly things that had survived my icy bath. I reflected that if I ever made it home, I would probably shower for days and never lose my joy of just being clean. I was so appreciative of the bath that I gave Commander Qasem my small telescope. At his request I wrote my name, address and thanks in his notebook. At least, if I didn't survive, someone would learn I'd made it this far.

# CHAPTER 10

We left Bozorq-Khel early in the afternoon a little cleaner but still hungry and hiked through terraced fields to the bottom of Teteen Valley. Like scrawny goats, we leaped over giant boulders and zigzagged across the same turbulent stream at least 10 or 15 times. I probably fell twelve out of fifteen attempts. On one tumble I tore most of the skin off the outer part of my right hand and knew such a deep wound would soon be badly infected.

By mid-afternoon we were out of the forest slipping, sliding down shale-covered hillsides and climbing precipitous slopes, but at least there was no snow. Scrambling through the shale tore my toenails from their bed, and I taped them back on during a tea break. After a too-short rest we forded a wide, hip-deep and freezing stream. At least this effort numbed my sore feet for a while. The current was swift and progress was slow. First we formed a human chain across the river, then had the men on the near side of the chain go across one by one in front of the rest of us. There were numerous falls accompanied by spluttering, screaming and Afghan curses, but I managed to do better than usual. This time I kept my shoes on to protect my nails and was able to get better footing on the rocky bottom.

After crossing the stream we squished along a good path for several miles to the road-side bazaar of Gandala-Buc. I was tired but happy to have survived another day and immediately fell asleep on a bed of straw. Just before midnight I was suddenly awakened and rushed to another hut. *"Beelah, putsha!"* (Hurry, hide yourself) was repeated over and over during the night while I was quietly shuffled from hut to hut. Nasir finally whispered that some "bad people" were searching for me in this village. When I pressed him for an explanation, he answered that at the last village I had written my name and address in the book of a commander suspected of KGB connections. I had identified myself as the American the Soviets were trying to locate. Now they would start looking for us with greater intensity. And I'd thought he was just being hospitable! To top this, for no apparent reason, I suddenly remembered today was April 15 and my income tax was due. This chilling thought had barely registered when Nasir again whispered "Come."

We glided silently through the dark alleys between the smelly hovels, crouching breathlessly each time one of the village dogs barked. The faint moonlight guided us out to the edge of the settlement, where we climbed onto an abandoned flat-roofed structure. I used my *pakul* as a pillow, wrapped my prayer blanket around me and fell asleep immediately.

Braying donkeys and loud praying awakened us before dawn, and we were on the trail before six. There was no time for teeth brushing, hair combing or any of the things I would have liked to do to feel a little better. This was particularly exasperating since we only walked about ten minutes, then stopped to rest. By 8:00 a.m. we'd reached a hilly road which had probably been a main highway in the past but was now pot-holed with so many bomb craters and landslides even a tank couldn't pass. We didn't fix tea but located a spring flowing into a small pool infested with tadpoles. I put my head in the water and sucked it through my teeth without swallowing any of the small swimmers. While we sat by the spring, my depression returned like a sodden blanket. My mind wouldn't leave the theme of how little I'd accomplished for the sick and wounded thus far and of the increasing probability I might fail in my effort to meet Massoud or get killed.

Then, like a weight dropping on my shoulders, I realized today, April 16, was my third wedding anniversary. We plodded on, and I swore never to be away from Pam and my family like this again.

I was lost in my misery when two Soviet MIGs were upon us before anyone saw them. We ducked into a crevice as the jets screamed back toward the village we had left earlier that morning. Baba indicated they were planning to bomb the village where we had spent the night, but I heard no gunfire or explosions. I was grateful for the break and almost welcomed the interruption of the jets, but I was still in a foul mood. When the MIGs turned for another pass, I ran into the middle of the road and flipped my middle finger at the Soviets as they roared by, almost at eye level with us. I'll never forget the amazed look of the pilot. The shocked Afghans screamed at me, and I realized how stupid I'd been. At least it relieved my depression. Fortunately the jets were not interested in one crazy "Afghan" and disappeared over the mountains.

Nasir and the colonel had left earlier that morning to explore an alternate route, so I walked along with the rest of the group who were silently furious at me for endangering them. Mid-morning we stopped at an incredibly filthy roadside store about the size of a clothes closet. Everything, including the proprietor and his one customer, was covered with flies. Therefore, lunch was obtained from our meager supplies. We divided a can of cheese among us, and for dessert each of us was allotted one stale cookie and a fig.

By the time we had finished, Nasir and the colonel had rejoined us and were promptly informed about my stunt in the road. Nasir thought it hilarious and said not to worry about the others' reactions. It felt great having someone to talk to after a morning of not understanding the group's conversation and wondering if they were going to abandon me for my stupidity and slowness.

Nasir told me we were now following the Alingar River and its valley. This provided a relatively easy trail, but there was constant danger from Soviet aircraft. Particularly after my dumb gesture that morning, he reminded me, it was important to stay hidden from all airplanes, since they could radio for the dreaded helicopters. No one could hide from those predators.

While tea was heating, Nasir, the Colonel, Naim and I went to the stream and used my small vial of shampoo to wash up. After the bath, I knew I was accepted as an Afghan, for the other men let me see them naked from the waist up, something they would never have done in front of a *ferengir* (foreigner). Naim not only bathed but swam in the swift current to mid-stream and back. He was the only Afghan I met who could swim or wasn't deathly afraid of water.

The afternoon was relatively pleasant as we followed an easy trail up and down hills beside the river. Sunlight faded. We crossed a small stream and stopped in a nearby village. Apparently this one was friendly, for I was identified as a doctor. A sick man was brought to me complaining of cough plus general aches and pains. I examined him but had no appropriate medicines, so I wrote a prescription which he tucked into his pocket. He vowed to take it back to Peshawar and have it filled. I'm sure the prescription served only as an amulet or placebo, but it was all I had and I hoped it helped him.

Suppertime brought a special treat. We boiled a chicken and before dividing the meat drank the water in which it had been boiled. It was only thin broth and tasted more of feathers than chicken, but at least it contained a little salt. The meat was rubbery and tasteless, but we ate it all. The Afghans even gnawed the bones. I hoped the alleged benefits of chicken soup weren't strictly a Jewish remedy but extended to "us Muslims" as well.

We were up by 4:00 a.m. and walking by 5:30 over a trail high above the river. The path narrowed, then descended to the river level, and rose up again. Baba repeatedly got lost. I grew frustrated and grouchy, particularly

Naim and I conquer another mountain.

after we forded an icy stream in water up to our waists. Although the water felt great, I slashed both my feet on the rocks of the streambed. I had taken off my shoes and hung them around my neck in hopes of keeping them dry for a time. A bad decision. As I limped along, Nasir compounded my ill humor by telling me my single patient last night was not happy with my treatment and had expected more. He was probably upset because I didn't have any pills to give him. At least he couldn't complain about my fee. I should have billed him for the world's longest house call.

We spent the morning enduring a steady uphill climb, then stopped at a small village just before noon. I was covered with flies, almost smothered by the odor of human feces, and sat under a tree surrounded by curious villagers as I added a few notes in my journal.

When we descended into the valley near the river, the heat was intense even in the shade, and all of us were dripping with sweat. We crossed a swaying lofty bridge suspended between two cliffs high over a raging torrent of muddy water, and I was reminded of the final scenes from the movie, *The Man Who Would Be King*, wherein the hero was executed on such a bridge. We were now deeply in Nuristan (Kaffiristan), the supposed locale of Kipling's story on which the movie was based.

During lunch—another shared can of cheese and some tea—I became acutely more homesick. My mind was filled with thoughts of Hayne and Pam, as well as dreams of all kinds of fast foods, snacks, and cold beer. All of us were extremely tired and apprehensive about a huge mountain to be crossed the next day. I wondered if I could make it. I had to; there was no turning back now.

When we rounded a corner of the trail, I saw the massive snow-covered crag looming ahead, its peak imposing and ominous above the clouds. We stopped for mid-day in a small village, and I treated a dozen patients who presented the usual complaints of stomach and muscle discomfort. I had learned from my experience the previous day, and I made sure each patient got a pill or two of some kind even if it was just an aspirin. After walking up and down hills and climbing pole ladders to visit the houses of the sick, I was worn out, but practicing medicine again helped relieve my depression.

In the early afternoon another crisis occurred. Some people in the village told Baba his home in the Panjsher Valley had been bombed. He quickly left us to check on his family. I was not sure any of the others knew the correct trail, and I feared without the old man's guidance we'd blunder around in this savage terrain even more. I never saw Baba again or learned of his fate.

At a small fly-covered house, the genial owner brought out his bashful blue-eyed daughter dressed in her Sunday best so I could take her picture. This shy little girl seemed about eight years old. She had a fever, so I dug out some aspirin from my bag and ground it up in a cup of warm milk for her to drink. Her smile of gratitude compensated for all of the miseries thus far. I felt happy again.

After only a short walk along the path, my good spirits were crushed. A portion of the trail had fallen off the side of the mountain, leaving a sheer rock face with a twenty-foot gap. Below it was a small ledge which we hoped would catch us if we missed our footing. If not, it was a *long* way to the bottom.

Nasir tried first, lost his grip and slid to the ledge below, badly bruising his hip. We were able to pull him back using our knotted prayer blankets. Then I began my attempt. I inched across, suspended only by my fingertips, surprised I had enough strength to move at all. God, it felt good to reach the other side. When I made it, the Afghans applauded. This was the first time I'd made a positive impression on them. Slowly and cautiously everyone else crossed safely, and we moved on.

Shadows were filling the valley when we entered another filthy village. All of the motels seemed full so I told Nasir I was tired of hamburgers every night and suggested that we should walk on for another hour or two to see if we could find a pizza parlor. My feeble attempts at humor fell on deaf ears. We struggled on past the place because, I was told, it was "unfriendly."

Every day Nasir and the colonel warned me about the KGB's presence in the villages. As best I could determine, the Soviets were trying to turn the various tribes against each other to avoid any coordinated guerrilla activity. Some villages were friendly;, others would have been more than happy to turn me in for the ransom or to appease the invaders and escape reprisals against their homes. To avoid any more of my blunders, I was repeatedly admonished not to speak to anyone unless one of our bunch was present.

We stopped at a barn for the night, but we had no food. My grumbling stomach sang me to sleep. It was a bad night. With all of us crammed together with the livestock, the room was stifling, and my sleeping bag was filled with insects of various sizes and biting abilities. For once, it was a relief to get up

The beautiful Nuristani girl and her father.

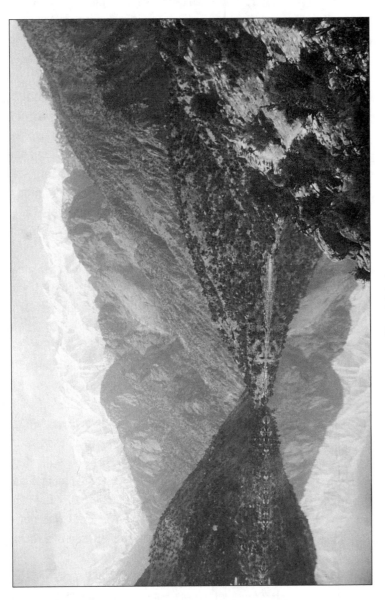

Mondul Lake

before daybreak and continue our endless journey.

We followed the trail up and down the course of the Poushal River to shimmering Mundol Lake, a view so spectacular it seemed unreal. The lake was long and oval with iridescent blue water that reflected the towering snow-covered peaks surrounding it. Tall trees arched over our trail. This peaceful scenery appeared far removed from any war.

All too soon we passed row after row of bombed-out houses littering the hillside. Pathetic, emaciated people lined the shore of the lake, occasionally managing to hook a few tiny fish. I didn't see a canoe, hollowed out log, or any type of watercraft in the entire area. When I asked Nasir why they didn't have a raft or boat to go out on the lake for larger fish, he replied contemptuously, "These are Nuristani, *kaffirs* (unbelievers). They are stupid." I wanted to stay and show them how to build a raft so they could go out on the lake and throw a grenade or do something to get more fish. Unfortunately we had to press on.

Our trail followed the lakeshore, then wound through a wide flat plateau, a perfect place for an airdrop of supplies or even landing an airplane. I made a mental map of this area in case we could ever work out a method of sneaking in supplies.

We reached a fork in the stream and were walking along the Linar River when we came upon a cadaverous old man with a young male companion sitting on a rock beside the river. The ancient, withered Afghan wore a sock on one hand. I motioned for him to remove it so I could examine his injury. He removed the sock. All that remained of his hand to the wrist was a black shrunken mummified remnant. He'd tried to cross the mountain pass we were heading for and gotten caught in a violent snowstorm. His entire hand had frozen. Now he was walking to Peshawar, hoping to get some medical aid. I knew the gangrenous hand was lost and would fall off long before he got there, but he was a typically hardy Afghan and would survive. But I was not an Afghan, only an exhausted, semi-starved American who would probably lose more than a hand in the snows ahead.

We left the riverbed to begin a slow painful ascent over rocks and cliffs, helping one another to a higher level. We waded several frigid streams, then struggled through another hand-over-hand climb. By early afternoon, numb with fatigue, we had reached the Cliffside village of Linar. All of our gear had been soaked fording a stream, but there was no time to stop and dry anything.

We continued to climb, passing awesome, roaring waterfalls. One I shall never forget. The white foam streaming over the flat rocks looked exactly like pouring milk. I stopped and stared for several minutes, imprinting the scene in my memory, then resumed the climb. We camped on a tiny ledge overlooking the river, wolfed down a quick lunch of more canned cheese, then struggled on.

As the day passed and we climbed higher, the temperature dropped precipitously. We could see a terrible snowstorm raging in the mountains ahead and decided to stay in the small hillside village of Shalidor with one of Naim's friends. Everyone was exhausted but exhilarated because we'd covered so many miles over such terrible terrain. I could tell they were pleased that I had hung in there all day. I knew in a couple more days the true test would come, but I tried not to think about it, filling my mind instead with thoughts of Pam. She was scheduled for her Cesarean section today. I prayed for her safety and that our new baby would be as strong, healthy and as great a joy as Hayne. How I longed to be there.

I was sitting off by myself, lost in thought and becoming very tearful, when Naim ushered me into a room in his friend's house. The villagers had collected lovely, white flowers from the high mountains and completely decorated the room. Pots of hot tea were steaming, and a small goat had been boiled. Apparently Nasir told Naim's friend my wife was having a baby that night and the celebration was arranged in my honor. That's when I really broke down. I wished I knew more of their language to thank them properly but could only murmur, *"Tashakoor, tashakoor"* (Thank you). Maybe my tears and expression spoke for me.

Since I was their honored guest I was served the goat's liver. This treat was distinctly under done. While I chewed, blood mixed with tears ran down my chin, but it tasted grand. Everyone was yelling and talking, celebrating loudly and I joined the fun. The Afghans made bets about the baby, wagering back and forth whether it would be a boy or girl. Nasir put his money on another boy, and we agreed to collect our bets when (or if) we returned to Peshawar. I fell asleep with a full stomach and a full heart.

In honor of the occasion, Nasir let us rest until seven the next morning. Everyone was in high spirits when we began our trek, but the day promptly turned sour. After prolonged and vigorous arguments between our group and some of the villagers who were trying to charge us double the usual rate for porters, no settlement could be reached, and we left carrying all of our own gear. We grumbled along for over an hour and were resting by a small stream when a horseman arrived. Everyone insisted I ride this beast with as much gear as I could balance, but the horse refused to cooperate. I dismounted, piled on our baggage and led the balky animal down the narrow rocky trail. When the path leveled, they again indicated that I should ride. Reluctantly I mounted the swayback critter and traveled a few meters when the saddle slid off sideways and I was unceremoniously dumped under the horse and almost off the side of the mountain. My appraisal of the equine species in general and this nag in particular echoed through the canyons of Nuristan. This time I insisted on walking.

By noon we'd struggled into the next village, and after a long *jirgah* new porters were hired. Nasir had scouted on ahead, so there was no one around who spoke English. The rest of our group went to sleep after drinking tea, so I sat, daydreamed and ate a little cold rice before Nasir returned. We moved out again and made good time up and down the trail, although everyone was grumbling about the excessive charges for the porters and the lack of hospitality on the last village—an unforgivable insult to an Afghan.

By four o'clock we had entered anther tiny hamlet and decided to stop for the night. Snowstorms on the mountain ahead had obviously intensified. The terrible climb, now to be attempted in a blizzard, seemed impossible to me. The Afghans seemed almost as worried as I. None of them had crossed this mountain before, and Baba was gone. Nasir reminded me that because of the severe cold and wind I'd have to move faster than I had on the previous mountains. There were no alternate routes, and we'd come too far to turn back. There was nothing left to do but see what the weather looked like in the morning, then make our plans.

The temperature plunged rapidly when the sun dropped behind the snowy peaks. We stopped in a little mosque and tried to build a fire, but only a few twigs were available, barely enough to provide a little light, not enough for warmth. We huddled together in the mosque listening to the wailing of the frigid wind and shivered in our prayer blankets. I ate all the leftover food I could find, hoping to gain some energy.

Nasir informed me our aim tomorrow was to scale Aryu Pass, 6,000 meters high—nearly 20,000 feet. The climb was practically vertical. Recalling data from my days as a Flight Surgeon, I knew the atmospheric pressure at such an altitude was one-half that at sea level, and supplemental oxygen was needed at altitudes over 3,300 meters. My chances of survival at this elevation seemed slim to none. Besides the altitude and the climb, I had to again battle deep snow.

Panic and dread surged through me as I recalled how snow had almost killed me two years before. It was the winter of 1983, and I was participating in a survival course at Yellowstone Park. A snow shelter we were building collapsed, and I was buried immobile for the longest fifteen minutes of my life. My companions dug me out moments before I suffocated. At the time I swore a solemn oath never to enter deep snow again.

In the morning I would break my oath.

# CHAPTER 11

*Fight on my men, Sir Andrew sayes,*
*A little I'm hurt, but not yet slayne.*
*I'll but lie down and bleed awhile,*
*And then I'll rise and fight agayne.*
—Ballad of Sir Andrew

Somehow, at noon today, high on a mountaintop covered with snow, my soul returned. This brief note from my journal dated Saturday, April 20, summarized the most dangerous and incredible day of my adventure in Afghanistan.

After munching on the ubiquitous canned cheese for breakfast, we began the ascent at 8:00 a.m. I felt great. Our first obstacles were rocks the size of minivans. The going was rough, but I was surprised by my stamina. As the hours passed, the boulders grew smaller, but the climb became steeper. Before we reached the snow line, I was sweating profusely even though I'd stripped to my long underwear. When we began crunching through the snow, my strength ebbed. I welcomed the short rest while I redressed in my *kameez*, field jacket and gloves, then we began climbing again. Naim had me hold onto his prayer blanket while he struggled upward. I counted my steps, trying to reach at least fifty before halting. The snow deepened. Fifty steps slipped to forty. Soon they dwindled to ten.

Now we were floundering through waist-deep drifts. Wet, sticky snow fell steadily, and the wind whipped it around us in clouds so thick I could barely see Naim, only an arm's length in front of me. I almost screamed in disappointment when we reached what I thought was the summit only to see another peak ahead. I began losing consciousness and would revive with Naim slapping me on the head and rubbing snow in my face.

Then I'd manage a few more steps or stumbles, each step plunging me into thigh-deep snow. At times I was unable to lift my legs out of the holes and needed help to struggle on. I was living my worst nightmare. Everything moved in slow motion. I could see only a few feet in front of me as the storm hissed

A prayer of thanks for surviving the climb, April 20, 1985.

and roared. Thunder boomed and echoed down the canyon. My eyes were level with Naim's waist as the incline steepened. I'd fall, lie exhausted until I was covered with snow, struggle upright, stumble a few more feeble steps and fall again. The snow was trying to kill me. I should have kept my vow. I collapsed face down, couldn't get up, and lay with my chest heaving, then eased into blissful unconsciousness.

Naim was slapping my face from side to side, and I awoke to try again. I could hear the ominous rattling of fluid in my lungs, sank to my knees and began coughing blood-streaked foam. At that precise moment I knew I was going to die.

I had developed severe mountain sickness—heart failure resulting from over-exertion at high altitudes. Without oxygen or a rapid descent to lower altitudes, few survived. I couldn't speak, but I tried to let Naim know I must go back down the mountain. He kept dragging me higher.

I couldn't see. I couldn't talk, and Naim couldn't understand. I spewed more bloody foam from my mouth and staggered aimlessly in the clinging snow. I was in my final agony, suffocating in my own secretions. With my last conscious thought, I prayed for God to put me out of my misery—or somehow transport me back to Pam and the children. Then I collapsed in the deep snow, closed my eyes and waited for the end.

Like easing into a warm soothing bath, a great feeling of peace washed over me. *Dying is not so bad*, I thought.

All became quiet.

As if awakening from a dream, I opened my eyes. I was no longer gasping. My sputum had cleared. I stood upright feeling a phenomenal surge of energy. Naim stared at me in horror like a man seeing a ghost. I almost tripped over him as I rejoined the climb. I marched past him and gained on the others. The thunder was deafening and the blizzard was worse, but I slogged through the waist-deep snow and up the precipitous slope unconcerned. The last few hundred yards to the summit flew by while wind-driven snow whirled about me. At the summit I dropped to my knees and gave thanks to God for my deliverance, still confused about my escape from certain death. The Afghans stood by awkwardly and prayed, anxious to leave this stormy white hell. When I arose and joined them, I felt as if I were floating. All of the fears and sorrows of years past had fled. The inner peace I'd sought throughout my life filled me completely.

Nearly frozen but still alive.

Thunder boomed like cannon on the peaks, and the sound rumbled and growled down the valley. The blizzard surrounded us, taunted us. We were forced to hold hands and creep in single file as we blindly plodded downward. The footing was treacherous; at times we dropped through the snow up to our waists and were knee deep in a stream of freezing water. Swift currents undermined our feet, making us constantly afraid of being sucked out of sight. But we held tightly to one another, pulled each other from the holes and inched farther down the incline. Despite this new horror, I was unbelievably calm and remember singing every word of *Onward Christian Soldiers*. Later that day I could recall only the opening stanza.

The snowdrifts on the slope became so fragile we had to roll down the incline to avoid breaking through the crusts into the freezing water below the surface. Part way down the mountain a stream of melting snow zigzagged across the slope. I sloshed through this hip-deep torrent as far as it lasted, for even this misery was less than floundering through the clinging wet snow. The blizzard continued unabated; the whole world became a blinding white mist. Sometimes we could only crawl forward, blindly feeling our way with our hands.

Nasir grew furious at my snail's pace and began taunting the "weak American." I was in no mood for his abuse and began screaming insults back at him. In a burst of rage we struggled in a frenzied attempt to kill each other. But the snow was stronger than both of us and kept us apart. We calmed down, apologized and became friends once more, united in our suffering. It was undoubtedly the most frustrating and strenuous experience of my life, but for some reason (the new peace?) I never doubted I would survive.

For several hours after dark we jockeyed our way down the storm-ravaged slope, soaked to the skin. Nasir, Naim, Colonel Osmani and I trudged along, barely speaking, senses dulled by the altitude, exhaustion and cold. The porters and the rest of our party were already far ahead of us.

We heard a dog barking, and spied a light on the hillside far above us. After yelling back and forth, we climbed the cliff to find a small cave occupied by an Afghan family and their huge, white shaggy dog. His master tried to restrain him, but as we got closer the dog broke his leash and bounded toward us. As exhausted as we were, everyone scattered. The scene would have been comical except Colonel Osmani badly wrenched his knee before the animal could be subdued. The joint immediately swelled to the size of a grapefruit, and he could walk no farther.

The cave was little more than a smoke-filled cleft in the rocks but was a blessed relief from the snow and sleet. Two women and several small children left the cave and moved to a nearby hovel while we huddled around the small smoky fire drinking hot tea and trying to dry out. In a recess of the cave darkness I noticed a small cradle I assumed to be empty. We'd been there perhaps half an hour when a baby began crying and was retrieved by one of the women.

I draped my wet sleeping bag around some rocks by the smoky fire and lay down in my damp underwear. The roller-coaster emotions of the past day replayed like a movie in my brain. What had happened to me on the mountain? Why was I allowed to live, and for what purpose? Why had the inner peace been so transient, for I would have cheerfully killed Nasir a few hours later? How could I bring back the feeling? I had no answers, but as exhaustion and sleep overtook me, I recalled the words:

*When I was young I dreamed of the many goals I must reach, the great deeds I must accomplish, and the important things I must possess. Now I know there is only one great thing—to live and see the great light that fills the world.* (Anon.)

Lost and dying on an Afghan peak, I had briefly seen that light.

Wet underwear, my wet sleeping bag, and a hacking cough aggravated by due the smoky fire kept me from resting, so in spite of my exhaustion I spent a long, restless night. The Afghan family reclaiming their refuge awakened us at daybreak. I put on my clammy *kameez*, jacket and shoes. Colonel Osmani was in worse shape than I. In addition to his swollen knee, he'd developed severe conjunctivitis, probably from snow glare, and could barely see. With his arms over our shoulders, Nasir and I carried him down the trail for over an hour. A man on horseback happened by, and we were able to get the colonel aboard for a ride down to the next village. The rest of our group had arrived there safely the previous night.

Villagers welcomed us into one of their split-level adobe-style abodes with great hospitality, then fed us warm milk, tea and bread smeared with a delicious pasty mixture of flour and grease. I was famished, since I had eaten only some cheese and a few dates during the recent ordeal. When we unpacked our belongings and spread them out to dry, I found a torn packet of a cortisone-like medication mixed with the few remaining tablets in the bottom of my bag.

Another miracle. I immediately administered the tablets to the colonel hoping the meager supply of steroids would reduce the swelling in his knee and eyes.

After I begged a pan of warm water I joined the farm animals penned in a ground floor room of the dwelling and managed a sponge bath of sorts. I donned a clean *kameez* and waited for my socks to dry. I was feeling good...until I looked into a mirror and saw that my eyes were nearly swollen shut from a milder case of the same snow blindness that had affected the colonel. My face was terribly burned and peeling from the sun, snow-glare and wind, but thank God my hands and feet looked okay. No frostbite. All my hard-earned muscles were gone, however. My skin hung in loose folds, and I could easily wrap my hand around my wasted upper arms. My ankles were beginning to swell from the effects of malnutrition. But I'd crossed the pass!

Nasir brought even better news. We were going to rest all day in Paryan, this friendly village. In spite of everything, I was alive, dry and finally in the Panjshir Valley. I couldn't help thinking, though, that I would never be able to make it back the same way, and hoped there was an alternate route home—if we could last that long.

We spent the day resting, eating and dozing. I was sound asleep on a pallet but was rudely awakened by a goat jumping on me. Even with my recent bath I apparently smelled worse than he did, though, for he left promptly.

In the late afternoon I walked to a nearby village and began to conduct a small clinic for the assembled Afghans. It was a frustrating endeavor. I had no effective medicines and could only perform a brief examination, then write a prescription to serve as a placebo.

My open-air doctor's office consisted of a box I sat on and another one for the patient. Clearly I was the greatest entertainment to hit the village of Areb in some time, for soon we were surrounded by all of its inhabitants and their noisy comments. Such clinics often gave me the surrealistic sensation of playing the role of a physician in a theater of the absurd rather than the reality of my current surroundings.

Just as I was finishing my last patient for the day, Nasir grabbed my arm and whispered in a strained voice, "Dr. Pres. Please come now. A person is bad sick."

Using my tree branch as a cane I hobbled behind him up a rock-strewn path to a dark cliffside dwelling surrounded by a corral packed with stinking goats. In a tiny room lit by only a solitary candle, I knelt by a ghastly pale young girl swathed in blood-soaked quilts. Her only sign of life was the flickering movment of her dark luminous eyes like those of a trapped animal. By her side, wrapped tenderly in a prayer blanket, was her dead baby. The mother continued to bleed.

Nasir whispered a few words to the girl's young husband, and I saw his face suddenly gleam as he realized his prayers were answered. Allah had truly wrought a miracle. In this remote mountain village an American doctor had appeared who would apply all his knowledge, training and skill to save his wife.

But I could only hold her hand and weep with frustration while her life quietly drained away and her spirit departed like a silken scarf on a gentle breeze. The look in her husband's eyes when he realized his miracle would never happen—his wife was dead—burned into my soul to leave it scarred forever.

I put my arms around him, and we wept together. I'd failed. This whole damn trip was a sham, useless. I wasn't helping these people. I had no medicines or equipment. How could I possible aid Massoud and his troops? It was a waste.

I stumbled from the room and down the hill, tears of anger and frustration flooding my eyes. No one spoke to me when I dropped to my mat in the corner of our room and covered my head with the sleeping bag.

What was the meaning of all this?

In a few hours I'd moved from a euphoric state on a mountaintop, aware for a short time that God had truly intervened and held me in the palm of His hand—to a fury intense I would have cheerfully killed my friend Nasir—to the utter despair of my failure as a physician. A door in my life had opened wide only to close tightly again. I could but hope and pray I might one day find that door once more. Maybe the next time, I would be able to keep it open longer. For now it had slammed shut, and I was left alone to deal with failure, frustration, and anger at the vacillations of life.

I regretted today and dreaded tomorrow.

Once again we were up before dawn and walked downhill paralleling a rocky streambed; by sunrise we'd reached the base of a steep hill. I was able to claw my way up about a third of it, held onto the packhorse's tail for another third, and climbed the rest. From the crest I gazed at the winding river below as it flowed through the Panjshir Valley.

Typically, the Afghans decided we would go straight down. I tried

Batman's method of running down the slope, but all I did was mostly slide on my sore bottom. I don't know how they managed to get the packhorse down, but he was there by the time I joined the group.

At 8:00 a.m. we celebrated our successful descent with tea and bread at the juncture of the Khawak and Panjshir rivers. Then we climbed up the side of the opposite hill into a cave which served as the local supermarket.

I listened to the proprietor's portable radio while Soviet jets screamed up and down the valley at eye level in front of our cave. The syrupy female English voice of an announcer for Radio Moscow declared the Soviets only wished to defend their homeland. They had no thoughts of aggression toward any other country, she said, as helicopter gunships swept through the canyon like lethal dragonflies. We heard explosions echo not far away, but our little group was too small to be considered a target. The sun was warm and I felt safe in the cave, so I brought my journal up-to-date and once again taped my toenails in place.

We left about mid-afternoon to follow a narrow path along the cliffs overlooking the Panjshir River. The trees had all been blasted to stumps, and every village we passed had been bombed to rubble and deserted. Not a single building was left standing. The only sounds were the roaring of the turbulent river and the wind whistling through the empty shells of houses. I don't recall seeing a snake, lizard or any living creature in that entire valley. The people were gone, the crops destroyed, the orchards dead. What remained were the graveyards with their black pennants slowly waving in their solitude. I beheld complete, utter devastation. Our porters and we were the only living things in this once fertile valley. The Soviet soldiers had been here.

At dusk we left the bombed-out road and hiked rapidly through a denuded orchard, across a footbridge and up a winding trail to a partially destroyed house and courtyard surrounded by scores of heavily armed *mujahideen*. After a few words of welcome, we were escorted to a poorly lit upstairs room and were given bread, hot tea and soup. I was dozing comfortably when a group of bearded men dressed in surprisingly clean Afghan garb burst into the room.

I and Masoud enjoy a short break.

# CHAPTER 12

In the center of this group, surrounded by *mujahideen* laden with grenades, ammunition belts and Kalashnikovs, stood Ahmed Shah Massoud. I recognized him instantly. The man glowed with charisma.

With his *pakul* tipped at a jaunty angle, he wore the traditional *kameez* under a fatigue jacket. A checkered kerchief of the same pattern worn proudly by Naim was tied loosely around his neck. His face was narrow, with darting sad eyes, a Tajik hooked nose and a short beard. Of medium height and rather thin, he nevertheless appeared larger than on the video I'd seen with the Gailanis. His men obviously worshipped him, as did all the members of our group. He was very cordial, hugging and welcoming them all. He greeted me warmly, his voice soft yet animated. He spoke Persian and French with equal ease, but unfortunately no English. The hour was late and he appeared tired, so our talk had to be delayed until morning.

I was ecstatic. I'd had made it. I'd met Massoud and we were starting our mission at last. I went to bed and dropped off to sleep immediately.

In the middle of the night I was suddenly wrenched awake by a horrible nightmare. I knew, just knew, something terrible had happened to my elder son John. There was nothing I could do but worry and stayed awake the rest of the night. Now my overwhelming desire to get home was tempered by this premonition of the terrible news that would be waiting for me there.

I welcomed the arrival of dawn and was up at earliest daylight on Tuesday, April 23, eager for my conference with Massoud. Our camp was now completely surrounded by turbaned guards who stood like statues. I washed my face in a stream, but my toothbrush was packed with the other gear off somewhere with the porters, so I began another day with dragon mouth.

Returning to the house, I was summoned by one of the impassive *mujahideen* to follow him. We strode rapidly along a barely visible footpath that entered a narrow canyon not more than 20 feet wide. Descending into the gorge, we crisscrossed a stream several times before emerging at the thoroughly bombed village of Moukni. I was left alone in an upstairs room of a two-story building to await Massoud's arrival. Colorful Afghan quilts hung from the plastered walls, and the floor was covered with woven carpets and soft pillows.

While I was arranging my notes, a flight of Soviet jets made a low pass overhead, and I was rushed to a hillside cave to wait until they left. Amazingly, we were not bombed or strafed though all the village anti-aircraft guns were firing from hidden sites on the peaks around us. Maybe the MIGs were only reconnaissance planes, because they made another pass, and then disappeared. I wrote in my journal and napped until summoned back to the conference room about noon.

Massoud appeared soon after, and although obviously weary, he was most considerate and polite. A local chieftain served a large mound of rice to our group and tearfully apologized for not having meat to offer his leader. Massoud motioned for me to begin eating, but I diplomatically indicated he should start, and so we reached an impasse. He spoke a few words to one of the bystanders, who promptly returned with a spoon. I guess he thought I hadn't become Afghan enough to eat with my hands. Through Nasir I explained the situation, everyone had a big laugh, then we dug in and quickly polished off the rice. A good start.

Massoud brought one of his physicians to discuss the medical needs of his troops with me. I gave the doctor my medical bag and instruments. The bag had been a treasured gift from a senior physician I admired, but I knew it would be put to good use here.

Massoud was pleased with the tape player and radio, so I had Nasir translate that I hoped the radio would bring him only good news. He seemed touched and was particularly happy with the extra batteries. Such things were always in short supply.

After these preliminaries we began our discussion. The need for translations made our conversation awkward, but Massoud couldn't have been more patient. I took notes as we discussed his free-flowing assessment of the war's progress.

In spite of poor weapons, primarily captured from the Russians and a few bought from the Chinese, he'd managed to shoot down thirteen jets and thirty-two helicopters in the Panjsher Valley alone. I was surprised to learn many of the Soviet helicopters were flown by women.

The *mujahideen* would hide high in the mountains and fire down at them, hoping to hit an intake port of tail rotor. They'd long since learned choppers were too heavily armored underneath to be brought down from below, but they were very vulnerable to fire from above.

At least 100,000 refugees had fled the Panjsher Valley, but many still lived in nearby mountain caves, refusing to leave their homeland or go to Pakistan. Initially, a group of French doctors traveled with Massoud, but as the Soviet attacks became more severe, the French had departed. Since then, he'd been using Afghan medics. Although he was very proud of his physicians, he recognized that their surgical skills were less comprehensive than those of the French.

They had no antibiotics, intravenous fluids, tetanus antitoxin or even adequate suture materials. Much of the time, wounds were repaired with dental floss or hair from the tails of horses. Blood transfusions were non-existant.

Amputation was the only remedy for severe injuries to extremities. These operations were performed using only local anesthesia or intravenous sedation. In spite of this crude treatment, Massoud estimated at least 80 per cent of those with amputated limbs survived to reach Pakistan.

All abdominal and chest wounds were assumed to be fatal. Other than giving them morphine, very little could be done for them. Victims were placed in a cave for five days. If they survived they were carried to Peshawar on the backs of other men.

I had noticed in the Peshawar hospitals that most of these patients had developed severe osteomyelitis, a bone infection which greatly prolonged their rehabilitation and recovery. Their mere survival, however, was a testimony to the stamina of the *mujahideen*.

Between 1979 and 1980, fighting in the Panjsher Valley resulted in approximately five hundred *mujahideen* and civilian casualties. In 1981 the Soviets mounted two full-scale campaigns. The first consisted of two Soviet and one communist Afghan division attacking the towns of Rokha and Anaba. These assaults were repulsed, but the enemy could not be driven from the valley.

The second invasion was a massive coordinated operation by many divisions of Soviet troops and armor. This battle lasted seven months, was extremely bloody, and ended in a stalemate. Massoud estimated approximately 1,400 of his people died in these two attacks, and more than 1,000 needed amputations.

Following these battles, a truce was declared that lasted until mid-1983. The Soviets then resumed their attacks, and the war had continued almost constantly since.

In a seven-month period between 1981 and 1982, Massoud's partisans captured more than 1,000 weapons, including three long-range cannons and 30 to 40 vehicles. In 1981, using this captured artillery, he destroyed 38 helicopters and fighter jets on the ground at Bagram Air Base. With longer range weapons, his efforts could have been even more effective.

From April of 1984 until March of 1985, Massoud estimated that at least 200 *mujahideen* were killed in the Panjsher Valley alone. Civilian casualties were fewer than in previous years, but only because so many civilians had already left the valley. Soviet military losses during this time were too numerous to be counted accurately. Massoud's men captured over 700 weapons, six mortars, more than 1,000,000 rounds of ammunition, plus 25 heavy machine guns and 30 radios.

Massoud spoke with obvious pride and emotion of incredible heroic acts by his troops against all odds. I thought the story I'd heard in Paktia of how the Soviet tank was stopped and its cannon removed was unbeatable, but another story topped it:

A huge Soviet T-72 tank had rumbled up a narrow road defended by Afghan rebels armed only with rifles. One Afghan concealed himself in a covered pit in the road, and after the tank passed over him he clambered up the back armed only with a knife and a bucket of mud. He smeared the mud over the view ports of the tank, obscuring the driver's view. This caused him to veer into a ditch and become stuck. When a Soviet soldier popped his head out of the turret, he lost it to the Afghan's knife. The Afghan then snatched the dead tanker's weapon and shot two more soldiers when they came out. But one Soviet had escaped through an exit in the belly of the tank. He sneaked up behind the Afghan and shot him. Before he died, however, the freedom fighter killed this enemy, and the *mujahideen* claimed the tank.

In early 1985 the Soviet strategy changed. Rather than battle-line confrontations, they razed villages and forced occupants into the cities, where Soviet control was more effective. A valley or village was selected, and the area was sown with mines and butterfly bombs so no one could escape. Helicopters, jet fighters and bombers then blasted everything in sight; the area was surrounded with ground forces and armor. The troops now moved in to destroy all life—trees, donkeys, dogs, chickens, children, women and old people. Girls were raped, then tossed alive from helicopters.

Wells and water supplies were poisoned, everything usable was burned, and young boys were shipped to the large cities of the Soviet Union for indoctrination. When I naïvely asked how parents could allow their children to be separated from them, another horror was described.

The Soviets would select a child, dip one arm in kerosene, set it on fire and let it burn until it went out. Then they'd repeat it on the other arm. This atrocity persuaded other parents to let their children go rather than see them hideously burned.

I asked, "Why kerosene? Why not gasoline?"

The answer: "It burns slower."

The troops then moved to another area, but only after they'd mined the entire area and booby-trapped the bodies.

The genocide had begun.

Massoud noted that Soviet weapons were excellent, and they could amass murderous firepower, but the average foot soldier was miserably provided for. Except for belts and boots, their uniforms were worthless. And captured food was so bad even Massoud's hungry troops refused to eat it. As a result, Soviet army morale was extremely low. They frequently wounded themselves badly enough to be hospitalized rather than fight or run the risk of capture. Most of the troops outside the front lines were also heavily addicted to hashish and heroin.

Massoud's troops had nothing but contempt for the average Soviet and Afghan communist soldiers, but they grudgingly respected the Soviet Spetznaz commandos. These were tough soldiers who could climb mountains with 30-kilogram packs on their backs and fought ferociously.

Early in the war prisoners on both sides were questioned then executed. In recent years, however, captured soldiers from both sides were sometimes sold for ransom. The Soviets would free an Afghan captive for four to five thousand Afghani dollars or some watches. Massoud would occasionally sell captured Afghan communists to get money for weapons. Troops from the Soviet Union were also sent to Pakistan for interrogation by the Pakistani government.

The many strange and crazy things done by the invaders frequently amazed Massoud. Not infrequently, his troops had reoccupied a village only to find the Soviets had locked donkeys in second floor rooms to starve and had obviously tortured chickens and dogs for no apparent reason other than base cruelty.

When I questioned him about the Soviet's use of chemical weapons, I was impressed with his honesty. He said he could report what he had seen with his own eyes and what he had been told by people whose word he did not doubt, but there were some rumors he could not personally confirm.

He had definite evidence of a yellow smoke used in April of 1984 in Shotal province that burned the eyes and skin. In Hasarek province canisters of white smoke were fired from cannons and mortars that killed all the small animals. Strangely, horses and cattle survived. Some bombs contained a tar-like substance that stuck to the skin and burned horribly. Massoud's troops had learned to scrape the material off with sticks, for when they tried to pull it off with their hands, it would stick to them and burn large ulcers. (I would suspect some phosphorus-like agent, since this chemical is known to produce such effects.)

Massoud arranged a future conference for me with his Afghan doctor to discuss medical needs and confined his discussion to military subjects. As our rapport seemed to be growing, I asked him to recount some of the Soviet atrocities in his area.

Besides the gas, phosphorus and tar bombs, he also described the widespread use of many thousand butterfly bombs and their terrible effect on women and children. I specifically asked if he'd seen a bomb disguised as a toy, as had been reported by some journalists. He had not personally seen one but had heard of their existence. The Soviets also occasionally used a gas that caused a small blister followed by an enlarging skin ulceration; other gasses caused severe tearing of the eyes, runny noses and intractable vomiting. Massoud had personally witnessed Soviet soldiers dousing people with kerosene. He remembered one particularly terrible episode in the Bazarak area that occurred during 1980 in which a group of 15 to 20 people was set afire. In 1984, Massoud's soldiers discovered a large number of corpses with their hands and feet tied. TNT had been placed on their abdomens, ignited and allowed to burn slowly into their intestines.

Although I was there primarily to determine Massoud's medical needs, I told him I would attempt to relay any military information he wished to send to those in America who might help him.

He told me recent information confirmed there were eight MIG-21s, 16 MIG CPOMs (flown by Afghans), and eight MIG-23s flown by Soviets at Bagram Air Base near Kabul. The Soviet pilots were based at Tashkent in the Soviet

Union but refueled at Bagram. At least 13 transports were housed at Bagram. Massoud claimed he could easily destroy all these aircraft on the ground if furnished with long-range weapons.

Additionally he needed anti-tank mines and other equipment that would enable him to engage the Soviets in other than hit-and-run battles. Remote control explosives would be helpful, but his most pressing need was for every type of ammunition, especially for anti-tank rockets, mortars and cannons. If supplied with light, shoulder-fired anti-aircraft rockets, he could effectively defend against the oppressive Soviet air power. He'd tried using SAM rockets but said they were worthless.

Mortars of a caliber greater than 85mm, larger machine guns, clothes, shoes, and boots, all types of personal gear, binoculars for distant as well as night vision, plus long and short distance radios were desperately needed. The few he had were captured from the Soviets.

Because radios were in such short supply, Afghan boys as young as six or seven traveled through the mountains at night carrying messages. Older boys carried ammunition and food. By the age of 12, Afghan males could easily fieldstrip a Kalashnikov rifle blindfolded and were in the front lines.

This interview was conducted with frequent interruptions for Massoud's instructions to his troops and commanders, signing messages, and dispensing money (he was also the finance manager of his army). He performed all these tasks, often simultaneously, with amazing composure. He never seemed to grow tired, greeting each visitor as if he were the first one seen that day. He made me feel as if I were the only foreign interviewer he had met, although I knew my only distinction was being one of the very few Americans to interview him and the first American physician in the Panjsher Valley.

While he was hesitant to discuss any personal data, I did learn he was born in the Panjsher Valley and was 31 years old at the time of our meeting. During his second year of studying engineering at Kabul Polytechnic College, he became disenchanted with the central government and left Kabul in 1973, six months after Daoud took power. He escaped to Pakistan and studied three books—one by an American—on guerrilla warfare. In 1975 he returned to Afghanistan. Soon after, he and his men captured about 100 weapons and began their campaign against the Soviet infiltrators.

Until 1978, he stayed primarily in Kabul, organizing the underground, then worked in the provinces of Konar and Nuristan. Since 1979, he had

The old warrior at Masoud's hideout.

remained in the Panjshir Valley. His father was a colonel, and several uncles and brohters were in the military. He was not married an never had been. As I'd found with many Afghans, he seemed very shy discussing women and promptly changed the subject.

Not far from our meeting place, the Soviets were preparing another attack, and while Massoud became more involved with his plans for defense, I began my discussions with his physician, Dr. Abdul Marouf.

This pleasant gentleman was 37 years old and a graduate of Kabul University. He'd learned surgery "on the job" and had been in the front lines for two years. The list of diseases he had encountered included the usual respiratory ailments, almost every tropical and subtropical illness I could recall, plus tuberculosis, malaria, roundworm, tapeworm and other parasitic diseases. Most of the troops had skin disorders, especially fungal infections, and many were partially deaf from the gunfire. Dr. Marouf had no vaccines and few surgical instruments. He had no laboratory facilities; therefore, blood transfusions were not possible. There was no x-ray equipment and no protection from gas attacks. Since the Soviets routinely poisoned water supplies, he desperately needed a water purification apparatus. Devastation in the Panjsher Valley had been so complete that wood for cooking fires was scarce, and kerosene stoves would be of tremendous value.

Each week Dr. Marouf performed four or five amputations, and in the winter of 1984-85 had done 205. There were many victims of frostbite. These unfortunates just seemed to survive on their own as they received no specific therapy. In the entire Panjsher Valley there were only seven doctors, all busy with frontline forces, so the civilian population was essentially without medical care.

Compounding other horrors, mental problems were rampant. Few troops knew the whereabouts of their families, whether they were alive or whether they had left Afghanistan. These poor men had absolutely no recreation. Both Dr. Marouf and Massoud pleaded for a VCR and TV so troops could have some entertainment when not in the front lines. All morning I had watched men wandering about as if pole-axed, blindly staring off into space and mumbling to themselves.

Although our discussion was grim and depressing, Dr. Marouf provided extremely valuable information for future medical planning. After our discussion, I thanked him profusely.

There seemed to be no limit to the hardiness and fortitude of these people. In spite of all their problems, there was no doubt in my mind—or in Massoud's—that their struggle would eventually end in peace. Without better equipment he had no illusions they could defeat the Soviets, but he firmly believed the Soviets could never defeat the Afghans, and I was convinced he was right.

By late evening I was exhausted and had run out of ink in three pens. I hoped I'd made a favorable impression on Massoud which would smooth the way for other American physicians. At the close of the interview, he agreed to welcome them, for he said he was now convinced Americans were interested in his struggle and would bring help.

I had accomplished my mission.

All day our conversations had been punctuated with loud explosions, and my jumping at the first few caused quite a bit of laughter before I learned the detonations were from nearby emerald mines rather than Soviet artillery. The only depressing note was learning we would have to return to Peshawar by the same route we'd used coming in. Massoud said there was no other way to avoid the Soviets. I hoped the knowledge that I'd accomplished my task and was headed home instead of into the unknown would give me a little more strength.

Without moving from the cushion where I had sat all day, I dropped into an exhausted sleep and didn't awaken until morning prayer call and the loud traffic of busy men. I finally was able to locate my toothbrush and scrub off four or five days collection of gunga, then spent most of the morning wandering about taking pictures and waiting for Massoud.

I felt so sorry for his zombie-like troops that I picked up a large rock and began shot-putting it, challenging some of the others to join me. They were so desperate for recreation that within a few minutes thirty or forty of them were standing in line, laughing and waiting to take their turn at the rock. We kept the game going all morning, then I left around noon to pack my gear.

I was finally heading home. And I felt great, even though I was experiencing a recurrence of diarrhea.

As we were departing the area, our group was invited to tour Massoud's cave hideout. This engineering marvel was concealed in a canyon so narrow it couldn't possibly have been bombed and could easily have been protected by a few men at each end of the gorge. His stronghold had been blasted into the side of a granite cliff and seemed impregnable enough to withstand a small nuclear device.

This fortress, carved from solid rock, was composed of three stories. A jail for defectors was on the lowest level. It contained twelve Afghan communist prisoners. Rooms for headquarters, barracks and storage occupied the second and third stories.

I was ushered into a large conference chamber to meet again with Massoud and invited to sit at his right hand while battle plans were discussed. I knew then I'd made a good impression the previous day.

The Soviets, I learned, were poised at the end of the valley, and Massoud was anxious for us to leave before any fighting started. We took a few farewell pictures and said our good-byes. I again promised Massoud that, *"inshallah"* (if Allah wills it), I would send help to him from America.

He honored me by replying, "When I defeat the Soviets you will ride with me on the first tank into Kabul."

Later as I walked along the trail, I reflected on how much I had learned. As the Soviets systematically destroyed crops and villages, Afghan families streamed out of their homeland into squalid refugee camps. From a pre-war population of sixteen million people, four to five million were now refugees in Pakistan, Iran or the high Hindu Kush mountains. Food as well as arms would have to be transported to the guerrillas over perilous trails while the Soviets poured in masses of materials by road and air. The Afghan people were willing to endure unbelievable punishment. It was unthinkable for the *mujahideen* to yield. There could be no surrender. I stopped as the chilling thought hit me, "My God, the Soviets will kill them all!"

In his account of the apathetic response of the U.S. government to the Holocaust, Arthur Morse wrote, *If genocide is to be prevented in the future, we must understand how it happened in the past, not only in terms of the killers and the killed but of the bystanders.*

As I began the long trek home, I vowed not to be a bystander to the genocide in Afghanistan.

# CHAPTER 13

*The lunar landscape of the Hindu Kush, as if borrowed from pre-history, seems still to be waiting for the birth of the animal world, or perhaps to announce its end.*
—Rene Dollot

Everyone was walking fast and as the light faded, we passed through the abandoned village we'd visited a couple of days before and moved swiftly along the bombed-out road. After dark we traveled by moonlight, scrabbling over cliffs, clinging to underbrush and hearing our mini-landslides echo in the Panjsher River far below. Without serious mishap, we made it back to the junction of the rivers where we'd entered the valley. After brewing tea, we spent the night in the dirtiest hovel I'd seen since Kor-Dar. I'd eaten nothing all day, but at least my intestinal problems had abated.

Up and on our way at a fast clip by 5:30 a.m., we followed the river valley for a few miles, forded an icy stream, and climbed a steep trail by the river, finally stopping at a roadside house for the inevitable tea. An elderly Afghan resting there asked Nasir if I was an American and, with Nasir translating, told me a story of the lone American who hunted Marco Polo sheep in these mountains many years ago. He was greatly respected by the Afghans who admired his bravery and stamina. Nasir told me later that this man was a former American ambassador to Afghanistan. He must have been an incredibly brave and hardy person to trek these mountains alone.

The tea warmed me, but as we began walking, I grew weaker and weaker. The poor diet and recurrent diarrhea were taking their toll. In a few hours I was barely able to struggle up the slightest incline.

Someone found an emaciated horse with ribs like a picket fence. Although I was afraid to ride this beast up the narrow trail without bridle or saddle, I couldn't climb another step. The horse plodded along at a vexingly slow pace up the mountain path, placidly oblivious to my constant kicking and coaxing. When we reached a cliff at the crest, my worst fears were realized—suddenly, the horse began to buck. I gripped his mane and held on until *he* fell down. Teetering on the edge of the precipice, I was thrown back on the path, more angry than afraid, and would have shot this nag on the spot if I'd had a gun. Nasir's bag and some of the loose luggage fell from the horse's pack down the mountain, so our hapless porter had to walk halfway down the steep trail to retrieve it.

The path had leveled out somewhat on the mountain summit so I stumbled along after telling Nasir I'd rather eat the damn horse than ride him anymore.

By noon we had arrived in the village of our recovery from last week's ordeal and were greeted as warmly as before. There was tea, cheese and bread, followed by a short nap, frequently interrupted by curious children and villagers.

One of the young boys brought a butterfly bomb to show us. These were old news by now, so I didn't pay much attention—until Naim suddenly grabbed it and tossed it through the open door where it exploded against a rock. It was a live one that the kid hadn't disarmed! A couple of jolts and it would have "disarmed" all of us!

Later that evening I heard the news I'd been dreading. Tomorrow we would begin our crossing of Aryu Pass—the one that had almost killed me. Our hope was to reach it in the early morning hours when the icy crust would be thick enough to allow us to walk on its surface rather than struggle through deep drifts. I took consolation in knowing the ascent from this side of the mountain would be a little less strenuous. I'd worry later about getting down the killer slope on the other side.

Nasir rented a few horses and promptly at 8:00 p.m. our long single file of riders and walkers left the village. In spite of my old army jacket and long underwear, I was freezing. Frost formed on the horse's mane and in my nostrils. My beard was stiff with ice. About midnight we reached the snow line, which was as far as the horses could go. They were taken back to the village. Some of our group wanted to begin the climb immediately, but Nasir insisted we wait a few hours to make sure a good crust had formed. A loud argument started, so I began walking around in the dark looking for a cave or a place to build a small fire. Clumsy as usual, I broke through the snow crust into an icy stream soaking my boots and legs.

The mountain was barren of wood, but we uprooted a sage-like bush growing between the boulders and built a fire. It produced a terrible acrid smoke. Still, we huddled close to it, trying to get warm, until we were coughing so badly we had to move away. The cold would drive us back, and the cycle would resume.

At 3:00 a.m. we began the uphill climb. Occasionally one of us would break through the brittle surface, but generally the ice sheet held. Initially I counted 1,500 steps before stopping to rest, but the allotment diminished as we struggled up the steep slope. By daybreak the summit was in view. I'd climbed unaided all night.

At last I'd been able to scale one peak on my own. In the first light of dawn the scene at the mountain's crest triggered memories of pictures I'd seen of polar expeditions. Our single file of men, heads bowed, trudged in slow motion while their clothes and prayer blankets streamed in the wind. Under a slate-gray sky the snow coiled around us. We could see only a few meters in any direction, but this storm was nothing compared with the blizzard we'd endured during our previous visit to this pinnacle.

Just below of the summit, I "hit the wall" and couldn't move another step. Surprisingly, Jawad, who seldom communicated with any of us, silently took my hand and helped me up the final 50 yards. A few days earlier, I had treated his severe nosebleed, and now he was repaying the favor.

When I looked down from the mountaintop toward our old ascent, I could not believe that any human could have survived the climb and knew without doubt that God had intervened to save me from the snows of Aryu Pass.

Nasir and some of the others were already stumbling down through the snow, occasionally falling on their faces and somersaulting to a stop. As the overcast sky lightened, I could see far below the heads of people struggling up the mountainside to cross the pass, and my heart went out to them. I shuddered, remembering my almost fatal ascent.

I tried to walk down the slope but fell every few steps, and was soon exhausted. Once again I lay on my back, pulled my old army coat up between my legs and slid down like a toboggan. If I got going too fast, I dropped my heels, dig in and slow down. It was a stupid way to descend, for there were rocks sticking up out of the snow—and many more just below it—but to hell with it. I wanted to see the last of this place *pronto*.

I rolled, tumbled and slid for over a mile while the shrieks of people I passed echoed down the canyon. At last the snow ended. I climbed to my feet and stumbled among loose rocks and dirt, falling frequently, but moving determinedly downhill. By 8:00 a.m. the incline had decreased slightly, and we began clambering over massive boulders until I was dizzy from exhaustion. Eventually we reached a narrow trail where I could walk upright, but it took me over an hour to stagger less than a mile to the tiny village.

I limped up a steep ascent to a tiny wooden mosque less than a hundred yards from the streambed, so weak I quivered with each step. By the time I entered the mosque, my companions were already sound asleep, and I dropped like a stone.

In less than an hour, noisy visitors woke us up and began to prepare tea. I needed sleep more than tea, so I went outside to lie on a flat rock but was immediately surrounded by curious Afghans talking loudly and gesturing toward me. They were probably trying to suggest I needed a bath, for flies covered me like a crawling blanket. I had a choice of enduring all this turmoil outside, or going back into the cold and noisy mosque. I gave up any hopes of rest, sat in a crouch and stared at my ankles.

Soon after midday Nasir and Naim walked to the village of Bosaydur and sent back a horse for me. About 3:00 p.m. we left on the 90-minute trip to join them at the village. I arrived tired, sleepy, thirsty, hungry and sweaty. After some tea and bread, I felt a little better but remained weak and depressed. My only consolation was surviving the pass and the knowledge that each step was taking me closer to home. Even so, I doubted I could walk much longer. My shoes were coming apart, my toenails were falling out, and my body had turned to putty.

On the morning of Saturday, April 27, the village mullah must have set his watch wrong or just decided to get a head start on praying, for his call arrived at 4:00 a.m. Everyone grumbled but decided it would probably be best to cover as much distance as possible before the heat of the day.

We were descending now, and the temperature increased by the hour. The trail went up and down, up and down, and we wandered off the route several times. At 8:00 a.m. we stopped to take our morning tea, but the flies were so thick that for once I couldn't drink all of mine, particularly after I swallowed a couple of the pesky insects.

We began hand-over-hand clambering down slippery cliffs, then followed a long rivulet that soon enlarged into a wave-capped torrent fed by snow melting higher in the mountains. I had soaked my feet in the first stream, and thereafter waded numerous crossings the rest of the day without taking my shoes off. I'd become accustomed to wet, soggy clothes and drowned smelly feet.

In the afternoon we stopped for lunch. The flies were still in abundance. I couldn't choke down my portion of partially boiled eggs, especially after watching Nasir and Naim eat several of them raw. From somewhere Naim had obtained a live chicken and for the rest of the day he and Jawad took turns carrying it so we could have something for supper that night.

I was amazed at our rapid progress. In spite of my weakened condition I walked much faster and longer than on our entry trip. My state of mind had a great deal to do with it, for coming in I had no idea where we were going or what we would be doing; now at least I knew that, although frequently lost, we were headed toward home.

My usual mental gymnastics were failing to keep the old brain from focusing on our misery. I began a new fantasy. Mentally I prepared a talk about my trip to our local medical society, then revised it over and over while we walked. At the end of the presentation, I composed a tribute to Pam and wept each time I replayed it in my mind, wondering if I would ever see her or deliver the speech.

We walked past placid, scenic Mundol Lake without stopping for tea or pictures. The water level in the lake and its tributaries was higher than we had experienced coming in, and wading through the streams was more treacherous.

By nightfall we had reached the mosque where we had spent the night of April 17. I went to bed pleased with the number of miles we'd covered without any serious mishaps. I was closer to home but still worried about getting to Peshawar in time to meet my airplane reservations. I wondered how Pam and the new baby were getting along and dreaded learning the news about John. A number of Afghans crowded around as I wrote in my journal, but they finally lost interest and wandered off, so we were all able to get some rest after evening prayers.

Sunday, April 28, was a very strange day with as many mountains and valleys emotionally as geographically. For some reason we were again rousted out about 3:30 a.m. The previous evening I'd thrown away my last remaining pair of underwear and slept nude. Naim shook me awake and forced a piece of cold chicken on me. I had to eat it while still in the sleeping bag, then wait until their attention was diverted so I could get dressed. Without underwear, I was now clad (or, rather unclad) as a true Afghan.

135

We were walking by four o'clock—up and down extremely steep hills. About eight we forded a wide knee-deep foaming stream. Clutching desperately onto each other, and with the grace of Allah, we made it without anyone drowning.

My feet were terribly sore and my toenails were barely held on by adhesive tape, so I kept my shoes and socks on. This technique made stream crossing much more comfortable but squishing up the almost vertical cliffs afterwards was pure misery. Without the colonel's help it would have been impossible. His eyes and knee had healed, and all of his strength had returned. He believed I was a maker of miracles. "Physician, heal thyself," I muttered.

At the summit we stopped for tea and some greasy scrambled eggs seasoned with green flies. I was able to get down a few bites, but grease dripping off my chin, plus crunching unknown material in the eggs, killed my appetite fast. I guess I had gone without substantial food for so long I was never hungry and had to force myself to eat anything.

The almost vertical ascents and descents continued most of the morning. About noon we arrived at a high suspension bridge over a raging river. Many of its cross-members and wire supports were missing, as were most of the handholds. The Afghans refused to cross. But I reasoned that if God hadn't let me die in the snow, He likely wouldn't let me drown.

I gingerly tested the supporting wires and slowly tightrope walked across. The rickety bridge swayed over the waves like a pendulum. Nasir couldn't allow me to out-do him and followed very cautiously. Batman came across next, moving in slow motion and staring straight ahead. It was the first time I'd seen him ever attack anything with caution. The others, after much hesitation, yelling back and forth and arguing, refused to come across. The porters abruptly quit.

Another *jirgah* erupted. As Batman, Nasir and I started climbing an almost vertical slope, we saw the rest of our group on the other side following a gentle trail. All day we struggled up and down cliffs enveloped in a misty rain, repeatedly becoming lost but frequently having a full view of the easy trail on the other side of the river. When I asked Nasir why we chose this side, he became very hostile and wouldn't answer me. Later he calmed down and said "we" had made another error. The suspension bridge had collapsed right after we'd crossed it, so there was no chance to return.

About mid-day as we passed through an incredibly filthy hillside village, I was offered some salty buttermilk and sipped it very carefully to avoid swallowing any more flies. This partially renewed my strength but not my spirits. Everyone was in a bad humor, and Batman soon left Nasir and me far behind.

Shortly after leaving the nasty village, we rounded a bend in the trail and saw sparkling water gushing from the hillside into a small field of mint. To me there is always something of magic and mystery about a spring. I understand how water oozes through the earth's strata to the surface, but such a serene sight in this remote setting suggested some divine hand had poked a small hole in all the misery of the land to let some beauty shine through.

I lay on my stomach with my face in the mint-scented water and drank my fill. Then I rubbed mint all over me to smell much better—for a few minutes at least.

Night arrived fast in this narrow valley, and it was dark as we entered the village of Dahan-Piar around 6:30 in the afternoon. The rest of our group had followed a much less strenuous trail and had been resting for hours. I told Colonel Osmani I would follow him from now on if the group split up again. The colonel heartily agreed and seemed very upset about the day's disagreeable events.

The bags with my diary and few remaining pills were missing. After an anxious wait porters hired by Colonel Osmani's group arrived well after dark with our belongings. My old reliable jogging shoes were slowly falling apart, so I repaired them as best I could with adhesive tape and string. It was amazing how much abuse these shoes had taken and were still serviceable.

On the easy trail, Colonel Osmani had met some French journalists en route to the Panjsher Valley. They had heard in *Islamabad* that an American, Dr. Pres Darby, was with Massoud. So much for our security! They not only knew where I was, but who I was. Of course, the colonel and his group denied any knowledge of me. The Frenchmen had taken two weeks on horseback to come this far from the border, so I wasn't as slow as I'd thought.

We had hoped to cover a long distance this day, but because of the foul-ups didn't make much progress. The streams were savage and difficult to cross. Our route was hemmed in the narrow canyon by almost vertical cliffs, so we were forced to follow the river until it exited these mountains.

In hopes of a cooling breeze, we spent the night on the flat roof of a small mud and stone building near the river. I ate a tiny portion of boiled goat for supper, and after the exertion of the day fell asleep without any problem.

My hitchhiking crawlies kept me scratching all night. We were up and hiking before the first rays of dawn penetrated the deep canyon, and literally clawed our way up the next mountain to discover a primitive road. Now we really began moving. I amazed myself with the speed of my pace, even though I was weak from hunger. As I was dressing earlier this morning, I was astounded to see how much weight I had lost. My upper arms were the size of my wrists, and all of my pectoral muscles had disappeared. The bones of my pelvis stuck out like two pie plates.

We moved along almost at a jogging pace until midmorning, then stopped for a short breakfast of leftover cold goat meat and a few walnuts. As would be expected, the Afghans didn't want to follow the road any more, so after this hearty breakfast we climbed up and down vertical cliffs cutting across switchbacks of the old trail. We resumed hiking along the road again, our pace so rapid we were almost trotting. I managed to keep up with Colonel Osmani and even passed a few Afghan refugees. Later in the morning we stopped briefly for hot tea and some stale rolls, then moved out again, traveling faster than before.

We arrived at Gandala Buc just after noon, covering more miles in a half-day than we had in over a full day going in. We didn't tarry in the village but took off again down a hillside across rocky cliffs into a deep canyon and crossed an extremely rickety foot bridge over a roaring river, then crawled up the opposite cliff.

At the summit we met a few goat herders who mumbled vague directions to the next settlement, but it was obvious we were lost. Nasir wandered off, searching for a trail, then returned, still lost as ever. Darkness arrived with thunder, lighting and wind-whipped rain. We stumbled blindly up and down hills. I fell several times, once plunging headlong into the river and scraping my right hand so deeply I exposed the tendons, but at least escaped being washed away by the flood. We never did find the village we were seeking, and finally stopped shortly before midnight in a lonely hillside hut.

We had covered many tough miles that day, and everyone was worn out, wet and miserable. Some of the Afghans brewed tea, but I was too exhausted to drink any and knew the next day would be equally horrible. We were once again high in the mountains just below the snow line. I took off all my soggy clothes and immediately fell asleep in my bag.

On this last day of April, I awoke early and dressed in the dark while the others were asleep. Our poor but gracious host brought us some very pungent goat cheese, bread and tea but would take no money. However, I did partially repay his help. He complained of heart palpitations and wanted medication. Although his pulse was regular, I had learned to always pass out some pills and gave him three aspirin, the last of my medicines.

In the first glimmer of daylight everyone seemed tired and sleepy. For at least two hours, we worked our way up a streambed, leaping and climbing over huge boulders. The trail, such as it was, was terrible, and I felt myself was getting angrier as time elapsed. Each member of the group seemed to go off in a different direction, yelling for me to come with them. Finally they all disappeared on their own trails and I struggled on, following Nasir, who stayed far ahead of me.

About noon we discovered Noor and the colonel resting on a huge boulder, waiting to tell us that we had walked all this time into the wrong valley. We turned around and headed back down without any explanation to me. No one would answer my questions. I became so furious I couldn't even talk to myself. After about two hours of stumbling, mostly downhill this time, we arrived at a branch in the canyon, turned left, and after climbing for another hour, found the village we had been seeking. Everyone was sulking and silent.

While we rested in a partially completed hut, the local village schizophrenic appeared. Before the war this unfortunate soul had been a highly educated man, comparable to a dean in one of our universities, but his mind had been destroyed by the unspeakable atrocities inflicted on his wife and children while he was forced to watch. He seemed to have the mentality of a four-year-old. After he brought us tea, he used a filthy rag to rub our scuffed and sodden shoes as if he were polishing them. All the while he giggled and mumbled to himself. As he went about his tasks wearing his cast-off Soviet uniform, I was acutely reminded how this war caused not only ghastly visible wounds but destroyed minds as well.

At least the crazy man got us talking again, and we stuffed down handfuls of rice and tea. A friendly group of Afghan refugees joined us, increasing the number of my fellow tourists to twenty-five. We left the village at dusk, climbed cliffs, leaped back and forth (and mostly in) swollen streams and stumbled over watermelon sized boulders. It wasn't long before I was dizzy with fatigue, but we continued until dark and still kept going. By now I was numb. Just before midnight we climbed a steep slope to a rocky cleft and all of us huddled in a cave about three feet high, built a fire, brewed tea and tried to dry out. My shoes stayed wet, but I was able to get my socks a little drier, put them back on and slept in my filthy, sodden clothes.

During the night more refugees arrived. Our group had swollen to more than forty people. The morning began with a steady uphill climb. Two hours later we reached a juncture of streams and stopped for hot tea, cold chicken and bread. We crawled slowly up the cliff-side, trying to bypass the snow as much as possible. The colonel and Naim had to take turns pulling me. I was dizzy with fatigue. We reached the crest by mid-morning. The summit was so narrow that I could straddle it and see jagged snow-capped peaks extending to every horizon.

Much faster now, we stumbled down the steep rocky slope through snow, then hail, then rain. The trail was like wet glass. Each of us fell several times, rolled down the hillsides, grabbing at whatever we could find to stop our progress. My knees and thighs became more and more painful as we raced downhill. The rain finally became so blinding we stopped in an abandoned hut until it diminished. My poor legs welcomed the respite.

At the base of the mountain, we passed through a small village, then walked on for many more tired miles to the mosque in Kor-Dar. I remembered this place as the dirtiest village in all Afghanistan and found no evidence of civic improvements since our last visit.

We huddled inside a shattered building and brewed tea as the rain poured. In spite of the flies and noise I slept for a couple of hours. At sunset I was awakened and told we would spend the night in Kor-Dar and press on in the morning when the downpour had slackened.

Through the mist and rain I gazed over and over at the mountains we had crossed, and still couldn't believe I'd made it this far. For the past several days I had been wasting away more rapidly than before, and I wondered how much longer my emaciated body could last. I would face anything to get home, as I daily grew wearier of body odor, wet, filthy clothes and no food. But I knew every step, however painful, brought me closer to home. This kept me going when all my other tricks failed.

We began walking before daybreak, and I remembered today, Thursday, May 2, was the day I was supposed to catch the plane home. There wasn't much time to brood. Our frantic pace, fording of the streams and the never-ending up and down of our path required all my concentration and effort.

We had only one or two episodes of confusion and lost trails, so I guessed our progress was improving. Everyone was moving at breakneck speed, especially when we hit a good trail. About mid-morning we passed the place where we'd spent a night coming in. It had taken us only three hours to cover the distance that required a half-day to walk before. Lunch for me was only a little chicken and tea, while the others ate a bushel of onions.

We rested at the small village of Gusalak, and I passed the time listening to a four-hour *jirgah,* mostly arguing about the price of porters. This was followed by a fast walk to Kandi (the village of the beautiful mosque where I had enjoyed the buttermilk). The local *mujahideen* commander insisted we have tea, then gave us the bad news.

For eight days intense fighting along the trail ahead had blocked this route, which was now firmly under Soviet control. Everyone was disappointed, but there was nothing to do but make an abrupt turn and head back uphill into the mountains and search for a new route to Pakistan.

Our entourage had dwindled to twenty. The new guide was charging an exorbitant rate, and there were arguments and loud discussions all afternoon. Even though the new guide had a crippled leg and used a crutch, he climbed better than I did.

Just before dark we slogged through a blinding rain mixed with sleet into the hillside village of Krapo. I was so dirty I didn't even want to be around myself. Tomorrow we would have to climb another mountain so there was no use trying to clean up; besides there was no place to wash unless I went outside and stood in the freezing rain.

During the previous day while we stopped in a hamlet for tea, I found a mirror and got the first good look at myself in about a month. I couldn't believe what I saw! My eyebrows had fallen out. I had lost most of my eyelashes. All exposed skin was blistered and peeling. Large crusted, weeping sores were scattered over my face and hands. My long, straggly beard was a mixture of brown and red, but mostly gray. It looked as though I was losing most of the hair from the top of my head, and the strands that remained were matted, greasy, and unkempt. The only place hair seemed to thrive was on my ears.

My injured right hand was badly infected, and I was down to my last two sheets of toilet paper. But we had eaten so little I'd had no need of my precious supply of this item for some time. The closer I got to home, the more I detested the filth, flies and feces.

In spite of these miseries, we'd covered a lot of miles in a few days, and I was pleased with our progress. The new route would be tougher but a little shorter and hoped to reach the border in two days. My shoes were coming apart, my clothes were torn, I was filthy and didn't know whether I could last. But at least we were headed home.

Our wake-up call was before sunrise. I had slept poorly and was already up waiting to walk again. The previous night a local commander had insisted we eat and stay in his tiny room, which smelled like wet goats. In spite of this new olfactory onslaught, my appetite had partially returned. I managed to eat half a bowl of cold, gritty spinach along with some bread. Sleep had been impossible as the usual loud *jirgah* went on until nearly midnight; then I flopped about in my bag, lying on a bed which sagged like a hammock, trying not to think of my dirty, smelly clothes. It had been a long night.

We struggled uphill all morning, then joined another small group of refugees and walked through a shady forest of huge pine-like trees almost as big as California Sequoias. The local people harvested these trees by burning out the base until they fell, then fashioned lumber from the massive trunks with primitive axes. They lived in small log cabins surrounded by lush, green meadows and the refreshing smell of pine. Their gardens were well tended; their goats were fat and healthy. The people seemed friendly, and I hated to leave this idyllic setting—an oasis compared to previous villages.

After a mile or so, we began a much more abrupt climb. Naim, Nasir and the colonel took turns helping me. The ascent was tough, but I didn't suffer the exhaustion of the previous mountains, and we finally reached the summit at 9:30. There was no time to rest since several Soviet reconnaissance planes were circling overhead.

We struggled down an almost vertical slope, then followed a gradually descending path through several filthy hillside villages. Everyone struggled along as fast as possible all day with only a couple of five-minute rests and a quick tea break in mid-afternoon. The spinach had passed through early in the morning, and I was certainly hungry for anything except the usual fare of tea and goat cheese.

As the terrain leveled, we came upon a stand of stunted mulberry trees. A few Afghans climbed up and shook down the fruit into our *patoos;* then we dumped the berries into a stream. Ripe mulberries sink to the bottom while green ones float on top. Green or ripe made no difference to me. I stuffed them all down. The Afghans were sure I'd become incredibly ill, but somehow my appetite had returned, and I was too hungry to worry about the consequences.

At dusk we bedded down on the porch of an abandoned mosque. For once no one talked much, as we were all exhausted, but we had crossed another mountain range and covered many miles. I had hoped to clean up a little bit, but there was no water near the mosque, and since we close to known mine fields I couldn't wander about the area.

I went to sleep again smelly as ever. I was consoled by knowing we were nearing the Konar River, close to the border with Pakistan. Perhaps we could reach the border by late in the evening of the following day—provided the Soviets had not cut us off again. My shoes, clothes and patience were worn out. There was no more toilet paper.

I wanted to be HOME!

# CHAPTER 14

Up and walking by 4:00, feeling weak, dirty and miserable.

This journal entry of Saturday, May 4, described my condition as we staggered along in darkness through muddy irrigated fields and fell over low stone fences with everybody in a foul mood. After successfully jumping a few shallow streams in the darkness, I tripped headlong into a deep one and wound up chilled and soaked. The Afghans received another American vocabulary lesson. Everyone seemed impressed with my eloquence.

At daybreak we arrived at the base of some large hills and had just begun to climb when exhaustion overcame me again. My legs had turned to mush and would barely hold me upright. I was towed by Naim, the colonel and Nasir in rotation. Each time I thought I'd reached the summit, there was another higher peak ahead.

We reached the top of the mountain at last, only to be greeted by Soviet jets, gunships and cannons raining destruction up and down the valley while shrapnel screamed overhead. Most of the barrage was below us, but we scattered nevertheless, hiding in caves and under rocks to escape. Mortar bursts were landing precisely on the trail we had just used. I cowered under a large boulder and kept my mouth wide open, hoping my eardrums wouldn't burst from the noise.

Now I understood why we'd started so early and walked in the dark. Mortars had been zeroed in on the trail. We would have been bloody scraps by now if we had tried walking it after daylight. Soviet fire seemed to be concentrated on one side of the mountain. During a lull we slid down an almost vertical grade on the opposite side and hid on a rocky wooded plateau. I could see the Konar River in the plain far below as the jet, helicopter and artillery bombardment continued. Unknowingly we'd stumbled directly into the Soviets' spring offensive along the Konar Valley.

Just below us along the river we could see the hated tanks maneuvering amidst clouds of dust. Their smoking diesel engines added to the almost palpable din. MIGs flew pass after pass level with our vantage point and repeatedly strafed both sides of the river. Lethal helicopter gun ships swept over us with their deafening, pulsating, unbearable roar. The downdraft of their rotors

The man who saved us.

enveloped us in a whirlwind of debris. I couldn't see anything. The noise from hell was so intense I could feel my skin vibrate.

I screamed for relief, then folded my body into a fetal mass and waited for the end. I bounced like a rag doll with each explosion. The air reeked of smoke, gunpowder and my own sweat. This wasn't at all like the war movies of my childhood. It stunk, it hurt. I was terrified.

Slowly the blasts diminished and rumbled away like a vagrant thunderstorm. We cautiously crawled from our holes and gathered like stunned, hunted animals under the dubious shelter of an overhanging cliffside.

Nasir declared we were trapped and would have to go back up into the mountains, rest a few days, then try to find another route out. I knew I couldn't last a couple more days. If I collapsed, the Afghans would try to carry me and all of us would be captured or killed. This was the end—and so close to the border!

Our salvation arrived with the miraculous appearance of two young confident *mujahideen* from the local area who knew a path through the minefields between us and the river. These brave men shuttled one or two of us at a time through deep gullies and beside stone walls, then concealed us in the tall reeds along the river.

The artillery barrage had slackened while jets and helicopters continued to roar overhead, but the strafing had not ceased. We remained motionless and well hidden. No one seemed to notice us.

From God knows where, an inner-tube raft appeared. Some men piled on the raft, while others hung onto its sides. I figured I would be less conspicuous in the water, so I clung onto the raft with only my head and arms above the silt-laden flood, and balanced my camera up on one of the inner tubes. We drifted down-stream across the river. Any minute I expected us to be bombed or strafed.

We struggled through the torrent, following our two *mujahideen* guides, ran across a rocky flat plain seeded with boulders, through more the minefields to another river and jumped onto a small ferry. We floated downstream, ground to a landing, then survived another dash through the mined flatlands.

Finally we staggered into the abandoned village of Babar Tangi. All the adrenaline of the morning disappeared, and we collapsed in some empty bombed-out buildings. We lay as dead men, listening to the diminishing sound of the Soviets' total destruction of the valley upstream.

Col Osmoni, Nasir and I back in Peshawar, starved but alive.

A few of our group built a fire and brewed tea. I was too sick, weak and exhausted to drink it. I knew then I could not possibly go on, even though we were so near the border and safety.

I was unable to stand without fainting and my ankles looked like overstuffed sausages. For a time I was left lying alone on the ground while everyone else searched for a horse, but the entire village was deserted. I lay where I had dropped for an hour or so, then was able to force down several cups of sweet tea and some mulberries. I stood up, took a few tentative steps and said, "Let's go for it!" I was determined to walk until I dropped.

Our route would cross a wide flat plain passing close by a large Soviet outpost, so we split into small groups and left a few at a time. I stayed on the heels of Colonel Osmani while we followed the slowly ascending trail for about three hours. All of us felt safer leaving the river and the intense activity there, but as the path became steeper, I felt I couldn't go much farther, much less climb the last mountain range ahead. When we reached the base of a mountain where we were relatively safe from aircraft we stopped to rest and brew tea at a shabby lean-to.

After wolfing down an entire box of stale cookies with fake banana filling, I was ready for another effort.

We followed a serpentine trail up the mountain, and I wanted to keep moving, for each time we stopped I would have greater difficulty getting started. In spite of my pleas to keep going, there were frequent pauses for tea, prayers and mulberries before we embarked on our final assault on the steep ascent to the border.

I begged Nasir for one final favor—just once stay on the trail and follow the switchbacks so I could make it to the summit on my own. He said, "Okay," but promptly went straight up the side of the slope and disappeared.

I was determined to climb the final mountain unaided, so I pressed on, counting steps like a man possessed and refused to stop for rest. From some untapped source blasted a burst of energy, and I ran the last hundred yards drenched in sweat, out of breath but exultant.

I'd reached the border! There was time to take only a couple of pictures and to offer profuse thanks to the *mujahideen* who had brought us through. They refused payment of any kind and returned through the horror of the minefields and shelling to their native village. I knew I'd never see them again, nor would I ever forget these brave men who had saved my life.

I couldn't hold back. I outran the Afghans down the slope into Pakistan. Two-thirds of the way I bruised my heel and was forced to resume my usual plodding pace. At dusk I limped into the village of Mitai, leaning heavily on my trusty walking stick. I felt and looked like a crippled old man, but I was safe.

After an hour of bickering over prices we roared out of Mitai, tires squealing, in a Toyota pickup driven by a young adenoidal Pakistani. Even my Afghans companions were terrified by his crazy driving and tried to get him to slow down. He ignored their threats and increased his speed. I feared we had survived all the recent disasters just to be killed on a highway.

Later that night we were stopped at a guarded checkpoint by an arrogant Pakistani who wanted to show his authority. After a fifteen minute delay for bribes and negotiations, he passed us through the barred gates. For three hours we raced through the mountains, down onto the plain and entered the outskirts of Peshawar. At the first roadside store, we stopped and ate like crazy men. I wolfed down tangerines, bananas, some type of spicy hamburger-like concoction and two or three bottles of an orange drink, but I still felt empty.

On our arrival "home" we learned that the Afghan we'd met high in the mountains had walked to Peshawar, found the safe house and gotten the message to Harvey Snyder to change my reservations. All was well. Harvey gasped at our appearance, took several pictures, then dusted us heavily with DDT while I read and reread a long letter from Pam.

Since everyone had made bets during the trip whether I would have a boy or girl waiting for me, all my companions wanted me to put through a phone call to my wife right away. I didn't need any encouragement. After the usual delay I was able to make a connection and almost wept in front of everyone when I heard her voice.

There was no baby yet. A month overdue. The Afghans were extremely disappointed and all bets were off, but I was ecstatic and told Pam to try to hang on until I got home. Hesitantly I asked her if Cathy was doing okay. She assured me she was. Dreading her reply, I asked about John. She replied that John was fine. But I really didn't believe her. I figured she just didn't want to give me any bad news over the phone.

There was no hot water, but at least we had soap and shampoo, so I had a long cold water scrub, then fell asleep about two o'clock that morning. I knew I was catching a cold; I'd arrived in Peshawar with one and would leave with one.

As expected, the feast of the previous night exploded through me before daybreak. Between frequent visits to the latrine, I returned to bed with my stomach grumbling. My nose was running, I had developed a severe sore throat and felt awful. I found some old books lying around and read quietly until the others awakened. Morning tea partially revived me just before a couple of American doctors who had recently arrived in Pakistan came by for a visit. They were visibly shocked at my emaciated condition. My jeans and tee shirt hung on me as if on a coat hanger.

Later that morning we rode downtown to the Pakistani Airlines office in hopes of getting my flight arranged. Abdominal cramps made my wait to speak with the snotty Pakistani clerk seem even longer than it was. He kept insisting that it would be at least Thursday (this was Sunday, May 5) before I could book a flight from Peshawar. I tried to explain that my wife was due to have a C-section at any time and that I was a physician who needed to be with her but got nowhere. Thoroughly disgusted and depressed, I rejoined Nasir and the other Afghans outside the office. So close to being with Pam for her delivery and now this.

When I told them what had happened, Nasir asked me to wait for a few minutes while he and the Afghans went inside to discuss the situation with the clerk. I couldn't hear what was said and wouldn't have understood the language anyway, but I saw the clerk's eyes widen and his mouth drop open. He turned back to his computer, and his fingers raced over the keyboard. In a few minutes I was waved in and told he'd just found a ticket for me. I would be leaving the next night. I shudder to think what the Afghans had promised him if he hadn't helped me.

In celebration, Nasir and I got our hair cut and beards trimmed; then I bought a fresh *pakul* to wear home. While shopping I became so weak and dizzy I had to catch a ride back to our house. Each time I passed a mirror I was shocked at my appearance, for I truly looked like an old man who had survived Auschwitz.

I tried to sleep, but as usual visitors with their loud conversations prevailed, so I dragged myself out of bed, ate some soup and immediately felt better. I was finishing the soup and hot tea when I was called to the phone and asked to come straight away to the American Consulate for questioning. Although the soup had revived me, I could barely walk but agreed to go.

Nasir and I caught a taxi to the consulate and were admitted to its walled compound. Nasir was immediately told to wait in the foyer during my interview. I protested such rude treatment of my friend, however, Nasir didn't want to upset anyone and silenced my objections.

The consular official seemed to be interested only in the number and location of any poppy fields I'd seen. I suggested I had information from Massoud that would aid the American effort in Afghanistan, but my offer was ignored. I was questioned repeatedly about poppies, where we crossed the border, who was in our group, and other data I didn't feel he needed to know. So I lied. As the interview went on, I tried to tell the man how weak and ill I was, but he persisted until we reached a stalemate.

To end the discussion, I proposed giving further details to someone in Washington when I returned to the States. He gave me a number to call, and I was promptly dismissed, almost fainting as I walked out. I was never offered coffee, water, tea or thanks. So much for my State Department welcome. At the least they should have been grateful I hadn't been killed, captured or otherwise embarrassed them.

Nasir was equally upset about his treatment. We were very unhappy as we returned to the safe house. No one at the Consulate offered transportation home, although we had come at their request. I managed to eat some rice for supper, then I dropped into bed and slept as if in a coma.

The next morning I was very hoarse. At least my strength was returning, and I began making plans to leave Peshawar. I gave my camera and all my American clothes and camping gear to the Afghans, as I planned to return home dressed in a new white kameez and a black turban fashioned for me by Nasir. I wasn't able to eat much lunch but certainly felt better than the previous day, and the excitement of going home sustained me through the afternoon.

Colonel Osmani had already left for Islamabad, and I regretted not being able to tell him good-bye. It was probably best, since I would have broken down trying to tell him how much I appreciated his saving my life. I think he will always know I truly owe my life to him.

In an old Italian ambulance, accompanied by Harvey, Nasir and several Afghan friends, I was taken to the airport. We choked through our good-byes. Last was Nasir. We hugged each other, crying. I was only able to say "*Tashakoor.*" Then I turned and walked quickly into the airport.

Passengers waiting for the departing flight began their evening prayer ritual and gave me dirty looks when I didn't join them. I didn't care. I was too busy with my own thoughts. My mind was full of daydreams, and I still couldn't believe I was safe and headed home. I wondered if I'd ever again see the friends of the past weeks to whom I owed my life.

When we landed in Karachi the ordeal of a very thorough customs inspection began. I was very proud of my appearance and of constantly being mistaken for a Pathan. When spoken to, I would smile and nod, muttering a few words of Pashtu.

A very haughty Pakistani inspector made me unpack everything and wanted me to pour out my honey but I refused. Then he began to examine each item in my luggage. I was smuggling a couple of defused butterfly bombs in my sleeping bag, so as he began to feel in the bag, I growled in accented English, "Now you will have lice too!" This ended the inspection! He also missed the contraband fountain pen-gun Colonel Osmani gave me. I had wrapped it in my shaving kit.

A little over an hour past midnight we departed on a Pakistan Airlines 747. An excellent meal was served soon after departure and I gulped down all of mine, even begged a portion of my neighbor's, then walked down the aisle asking for leftovers from other passengers. My weird appearance and requests so frightened them I was never refused. I couldn't sleep and daydreamed until we landed in Dubai about four in the morning. We weren't allowed to leave the plane, but through the window I could see the terminal building, an elegant white marble structure demonstrating the wealth of this oil-rich city.

Diarrhea struck again, and one of the cleaning men on board wouldn't let me into the john. I couldn't explain my situation, so just had to pick him up and set him off to one side, step in and lock the door. The subsequent rumbling sounds I'm sure convinced him of my need for haste. He gave me no trouble when I exited.

We flew on through the night, reaching Cairo at dawn. As we circled, I was disappointed that I couldn't see the pyramids, but was just as happy we would not be spending any time in Egypt. From the air it looked hot, dirty and unappealing. We didn't leave the plane while it was refueled, then took off for Paris.

Time passed quickly, and another delicious meal was served—no flies, hair or sand in the food. I was becoming accustomed to this luxury.

Again I ate all of my meal, some of my neighbor's, and all I could forage from trips up and down the aisles. The young Pakistani sitting next to me became very friendly when he realized I was not to be feared as a fierce Afghan but was only a harmless starving American on his way home.

From the air Paris was the most captivating city I had ever seen. We floated over tall cathedrals, ancient bridges arching over the rivers, and wide avenues. The city of lights. It seemed to glow in the glimmer of dawn.

While the plane refueled, I enjoyed a stroll through the airport terminal but soon received a sample of French *hauteur*. An over-dressed and elderly French woman with plucked eyebrows and garish, thick makeup kept staring at me, then said loudly, "*Mon Dieu!*"

I bowed very low, without a trace of a smile, and answered her, "*Merci, Madame.*"

With great dignity I turned and reboarded the plane for the overnight flight to New York. I was too excited to sleep. Unbelievably, the movie once again was *Romancing the Stone*. By now I could almost recite the dialogue. I couldn't find anything to read. My adjacent fellow passengers wanted to sleep so I lay back and began recalling the sights, sounds, smells and feelings of Afghanistan:

—An oilcloth spread on the floor in front of your cushions with the tortilla-like *nan*, dealt out like edible playing cards.

—The early morning wake-up call when I felt like throwing a tantrum and screaming, "I don't want to climb any more...I don't want to walk any more...I don't want to MOVE any more!" but still had to get up and press on.

—Washing up as they did before prayer, then praying off at the side by myself, yet all of us seemingly praying together. As Nasir had said, "We all have one God, only different messengers."

—How I had adopted the custom of hugging other men and kissing them on the cheeks, and how strange it would seem not to do this when I got home.

—How it would be to look women in the eye and speak to them without expecting them to duck their heads, turn the other way and avoid a direct gaze.

—Exhaustion to the point of collapse several times a day, day after day, and the feeling of futility. "Am I helping or is this effort all wasted?"

—The always present love of my home and family like no other time in my life, and the return of my soul in a site so remote as to defy description.

—Sitting for long hours not understanding a word being said, not knowing whether I was being sold to the Soviets, praised as a hero—or just being ignored.

　　—The pride of young *mujahideen* with their captured Soviet weapons, boots and belts going into battle *knowing* they would win.

　　—That never-to-be-forgotten sight of a lone woman wandering sadly through the mountain graveyard.

　　—The odd sound of an Afghan with a cleft lip and palate speaking Pashtu.

　　—The God-like rumble of loud thunder in a blinding blizzard at a summit.

　　—The heart-rending sound of a strangling, exhausted camel.

　　—The experience of total deodorant failure and the constant sour smell of my own sweat.

　　—The odor of socks worn wet for a week.

　　—Struggling and sweating up a mountainside to reach a serene, level meadow cooled by gentle winds, then a walk through fields of mint.

　　—The wonderful pungent smell of gunpowder in the air, knowing that the enemy had again fired—and missed.

　　—The sure and certain knowledge that for a very brief time, high on a mountain in Afghanistan—God had held me in the palm of His hand.

　　I reminisced for hours over friends and enemies who would stay in my mind forever. I might have dreamed some of this for I had undoubtedly dozed a bit. When I came out of my reverie we were above barren stretches of New-foundland and soon landed in New York.

　　Going through customs I heard two elderly gay men loudly discussing my appearance, presumed nationality and probable occupation. I was tempted to shock them by answering in English, but decided to let the ruse continue. I never admitted I understood every word they were saying about me.

　　Probably because of my strange appearance, I was waved through customs and the passport office without delay and onto the bus from JFK to LaGuardia. I had difficulty adapting to conversation in English and answered questions after long pauses before I could get my mental computer going to reply. There was barely time to quaff down a cold beer (much better than the Pakistani brand), then I was off to Dallas.

　　I must have slept almost the whole flight, for it seemed I'd hardly settled in my seat when we were alerted to fasten our seat belts for landing.

No one seemed to take notice of my strange appearance as I rushed through the terminal. Even on the commuter flight to San Angelo, the skinny, turbaned, bearded person attracted no special interest.

From the air at night the twinkling lights of San Angelo looked glorious. I was home! Pam was waiting for me when I walked into the terminal. She was hugely pregnant and wore a hairdo that looked like the George Washington portrait on a dollar bill. As we hugged and began crying, I blurted out, "You look awful!"

"You do too!" Pam sobbed. "There's nothing left of you."

"Well, there's enough of you for both of us," I joked as we walked to the car.

I hadn't forgotten how to drive, but the steering wheel was on the left side. I felt I was driving on the "wrong" side of the road all the way home.

"Pam, do you remember the dream I had before I left?" I asked hesitantly.

"The one about the man with acromegaly?"

"Yes, Yes. Thank God I haven't lost my mind."

Then I told her the story.

In the carport Pam sprayed me thoroughly with a delousing agent before I made a bee line for the shower. I shampooed and scrubbed myself over and over in an ecstasy of hot water and lather, shaved my beard and couldn't believe my appearance. I hadn't seen myself full length in months and was horrified. I'd lost over thirty-five pounds and looked as if someone had sucked everything out from under my skin, leaving it hanging in great folds. My cheeks were concave. My face was only a jaw, a nose, and sunken eyes without eyebrows or lashes. When I unrolled the Afghan carpet and gave it to Pam, I'm certain I must have looked like a starved proprietor of one of the booths in the Peshawar bazaar rather than her husband.

I couldn't sleep, so Pam and I talked until dawn. Hayne woke up and wasn't quite sure who I was. I surely couldn't blame him, but at least we were all together again. I was home, safe at last. Pam finally convinced me John was fine, and the horrible nightmare of his death was only a bad dream after all. At last I relaxed and slept soundly. Little did I know that my work for Afghanistan had only begun.

# CHAPTER 15

I was home. I was safe. Our baby had not arrived. John was well, and I'd survived the adventure of a lifetime. I should have been elated but was profoundly depressed. I'd done so little for the Afghans who saved me. And here I was back at home recovering from the ordeal while they were still struggling. But it was time for me to try to get my own life back in order so I could then more effectively help the Afghans. Late in the evenings I returned to my medical office and dug through two months of paperwork. I dictated long overdue letters and made preparations to see patients again.

In the process I chanced on a very complimentary article in our local newspaper about a patient I'd treated. I dropped by the office of the San Angelo *Standard-Times* and left a thank-you note for the author of the article, Suzy McAuliffe. In the note I mentioned just returning from Afghanistan and would be happy to discuss the experience with her.

Suzy interviewed me, and her article was front-page news on May 17, 1985. On that same day my daughter, Mary, was delivered by C-section and was promptly nicknamed "Shala."

Suzy's article was picked up by the national wire services and published throughout the country. This was a good start for my plan to bring news of Afghanistan to the American people.

At Dr. Simon's request I wrote a detailed report of my experiences and recommendations for the International Medical Corps. I emphasized that any future medical personnel sent to Afghanistan should be young and single. I could readily testify it was no place for an old married man.

As requested by the consulate in Peshawar, I contacted the State Department in Washington but received a rather abrupt brush-off. However, I was invited by the Committee for a Free Afghanistan to come to Washington and present my findings.

In early June I was graciously received by Mary Spencer, one of the Chairpersons of the Committee, who had arranged interviews with various legislators and government officials interested in the Afghan cause. While I was there, I finally met Bob Simon after our many phone and letter communications. Bob was trying to obtain financial aid from the government for his International Medical Corps and was slowly gaining the attention of legislators who could help him. During our brief meeting we discussed his and my recent experiences in Afghanistan and how we could best publicize our information.

I was appalled by the lack of interest of the American media in the Afghan situation. Although I was interviewed at length by *Time* magazine for a proposed article on conditions in Afghanistan, it was never published. The editors replaced it with the more newsworthy problem of whether Americans were going to choose new Coca-Cola or retain the old classic formula.

Rather than trying to help the Afghans, it seemed many of the media people were afraid to offend the Russians by disclosing the atrocities I'd witnessed and refused to admit the existence of the butterfly bomb I had smuggled home. Still, I left Washington knowing I had opened some doors, for more military aid was targeted for the Afghan resistance. At least some of the legislators were interested in their struggle.

I also believed some of the information I had obtained, particularly military information from Massoud, should in some fashion be conveyed to those who could more directly provide aid to him and his followers.

Again with Ted's invaluable assistance, I was put in touch with members of the Central Intelligence Agency to whom I relayed as much information as I thought would be helpful to them. At one time Ted had served as bodyguard for Mr. George Bush during Mr. Bush's tenure as Director of the Agency. He was therefore able to connect me with then Vice President Bush's office, and my findings were detailed there also.

Flying back to San Angelo, I realized I'd probably exhausted all of my contacts in official Washington. Since the news media seemed to show very little interest in my story, I decided to begin a "grass roots" campaign to present my findings directly to the people.

Always in the past I'd been a very reluctant public speaker, but because of local interest in *San Angelo Physician Does Crazy Thing*, I began to receive invitations to speak at various service clubs in the San Angelo area.

Instead of avoiding such invitations, as I would have done before my trip, I began to solicit them. On each occasion I promised to be a unique speaker in that I would eat very little, charge them nothing for the presentation and would not ask for contributions. At the end of every talk I made a plea for everyone to write his or her Congressman, favorite newsmagazine, newspaper or television station and ask why there was not more information about Afghanistan.

With help from the Committee for a Free Afghanistan, my reputation began to spread. I was invited to speak in many parts of the country beginning in Reno, Bloomington, Dallas, Houston, Chicago and other large cities. With each presentation my delivery improved, interest grew, and always the message overcame the inadequacies of the messenger. Soon I began to experience the joy and power of moving an audience with my story.

In June 1985, Stan's documentary, "An American Doctor in Afghanistan," was completed and I was invited to its premiere and fund-raising banquet in Sacramento. I was given a videotape copy and was amazed to see the coherent and affecting story he and Emory had made.

It began with Stan's summary of the war narrated from the television studio, then should scenes of the *mujahideen*, our work in the refugee camps and the trip to Paktia. I was seen working in the outdoor clinics we established, even riding the hated horses.

The scenes refreshed many memories, but I had the eerie sensation that my whole experience of the past months was a movie and I had not lived the story at all.

The film was a great success and later was honored as one of the top documentaries of the year in California. This was obviously a tribute to Stan's abilities and film editing rather than my participation, for it remains my only starring role. My career as an international sex symbol quietly died with a single effort.

The progress of my campaign to alert the American public about the genocide in Afghanistan was maddeningly slow. I agonized that all resisting Afghans would be killed or forced to become refugees unless we could alert the people of the United States soon. I also knew Americans would demand support for the Afghan effort if they could only be made aware of the situation.

One steamy hot July day I was performing a flight physical on an old friend and pilot, Ben Keel. As usual we were talking about planes and war. Suddenly I yelled, "The Doolittle Raid!" This spectacular bombing attack on Tokyo early in 1942 by carrier-based planes brought hope and inspiration to the American people, who had received consistently bad news about the war until then.

I remembered the flat plain near Mondul Lake, an excellent site for an airdrop of supplies. If we could pull off this stunt and film the action, the American media couldn't ignore such a story. And we would be thumbing our noses at the Soviets. Fortuitously, Ben had flown into Afghanistan many times and knew the terrain. Better yet, he had kept his old maps. We began to hatch a plan.

We would buy a small twin-engine plane that would meet our needs. Ben would fly us to Pakistan and use our plane very legitimately to ferry supplies between the Afghan refugee camps. But on board would be a Russian-speaking passenger (I planned to use Colonel Osmani) monitoring Soviet radio transmissions to determine if they paid any attention to our flights closer and closer to the border. If not, we would load the plane with medical supplies, take along a professional photographer (Emory Clay?) to film the mission and zap in and out at low altitude.

We located a suitable plane with a sale price of $80,000 and hoped to resell it after the flight (if we survived) to recoup some of the cost. Other expenses were itemized to a total of one hundred sixty thousand dollars. I presented my proposal to the CIA.

They immediately advised me that we could only carry humanitarian supplies. Any military hardware would violate the Neutrality Act and we would be imprisoned for a long time. We agreed and were told to "Go for it", but we would be on our own. The CIA would support our efforts, but they wouldn't fund or acknowledge the project. The plan died for lack of money. I still think it would have worked.

I refused to give up. I continued speaking whenever and wherever listeners could be found. Sometimes the audience would be six or seven bored teenagers at a church Sunday school. Other times I received a standing ovation from hundreds of enthusiastic senior citizens.

On some occasions I felt as if I was speaking in a foreign tongue, for all the reaction I elicited from the audience. Other times I shall never forget.

Once I was the after-dinner speaker at the community center in a small West Texas town. I gave my spiel, showed my slides and ended my talk staring into rows of bored impassive faces. I was collecting my notes and preparing to leave, convinced I'd wasted my time and theirs, when I received a gentle tap on my shoulder. I turned, and the Hispanic cook with tears in her eyes pressed a wrinkled $5.00 bill in my hand. "Send this to the Afghan children," she said. "God bless you."

About a month after I'd spoken to a class of seemingly unimpressed and restless teenagers at one of San Angelo's junior high schools, I got a telephone call from their teacher, Mrs. Carolyn Underwood. She asked that I stop by her office to see something her students had done. I expected to see a poster or collage constructed, probably grudgingly, as a class project. What I discovered astounded me.

With Mrs. Underwood's guidance, these young men and women had written, produced and filmed a movie about the Afghan struggle and its importance to Americans. The videotape was shown widely to audiences in San Angelo, then the students raised money to take their movie to Washington. Their project was viewed by many members of Congress and ultimately was very influential in gaining these legislators' support for the Afghan cause.

These students and Mrs. Underwood helped turn the tide of public support for the *mujahideen* and contributed significantly to their ultimate victory over the Soviets. God bless them.

In September I was invited to give my talk to our local medical society, and for the occasion wives of the members were invited. This seemed to be an excellent time to deliver my tribute to Pam. Without warning her, at the close of the speech I said:

"In Afghan culture, public display of affection is not only acceptable but encouraged. So as a semi-Afghan and at the risk of embarrassing the person involved, I would like to demonstrate that custom.

"It is said that behind every man's success is a supportive wife, and a totally amazed mother-in-law. I don't know about her mother's reaction, but any success I achieved in my venture would not have happened without Pam's support.

"Some years ago, Pam saved my life, not in dramatic fashion as one would rescue a man from drowning; but she slowly pulled me from the far more treacherous waters of despair, loneliness and anger. And in doing so she showed me that there is truly life after death; at least in the sense that one must go on living, and loving, and striving, even when the loss of someone close causes one's whole world to collapse.

"So I say to you, Pam, 'Thank You, I love you,' and as it says on our sundial, 'Grow old along with me, the best is *yet* to be.'"

As I continued to travel and talk the trickle of letters and calls steadily increased, then began to pour into Washington and to the news media.

Legislators were kept aware of the public's interest in Afghanistan, and largely through the untiring efforts of such dedicated men as Senator Gordon Humphrey and Congressman Charles Wilson, the Afghans obtained substantial military aid. The tide of the war began to turn. For the first time it seemed the Afghan people not only had a chance to survive but that a negotiated peace was possible.

Late in the summer of 1985, another group of American doctors embarked for Afghanistan. All were young and single as I had recommended to Dr. Simon. They were also incredibly lucky. One group was attacked by helicopter-borne Soviet commandos in southern Afghanistan and barely escaped. A journalist with them, Mr. Charles Thornton, was killed.

Dr. Ron Halbert, a physician from San Antonio, along with an emergency medical technician from California, Jim Lindelof, entered the Panjshir Valley and provided invaluable medical assistance to Massoud's army. Soon after Ron and Jim's return to the U.S., the International Medical Corps received a grant from the State Department with the understanding that the IMC would no longer send American medical personnel into Afghanistan. This ended the clandestine infiltration by American doctors and nurses, and that chapter of the IMC's history drew to a close.

With grant money, the school in Peshawar to train Afghan medics in basic medical and surgical skills was greatly enlarged. After completing an intensive course lasting six weeks these men returned to the front and performed superbly. For the rest of the war, they provided the only significant medical care for the freedom fighters.

Largely through the coordinated efforts of the Committee for a Free Afghanistan and sympathetic legislators in Congress a program was established that brought Afghan wounded to hospitals in the United States.

St. John's, one of the hospitals in San Angelo, volunteered to participate in the program. I arranged for a young boy, Amanullah Khan, and one of the *mujahideen*, Major Gulabbidin, to receive care here.

Amanullah had sustained severe pelvic wounds from a bomb explosion and had been treated primarily with liberal doses of morphine. We instituted the initial repair of his grievous wounds and freed him from the grasp of morphine; then, after several weeks, transferred him to a medical center in Sacramento for rehabilitative care. Eventually he rejoined his family in Peshawar.

Major Gulabbidin, a handsome man in his late 20s, had advanced bladder cancer, an unusual disease in one so young. He had been exposed to some of the Soviet chemical warfare agents. Although it could not be proved, these toxins may have precipitated his illness.

For over a year he lived in St. John's Hospital while receiving chemotherapy. He quickly became the center of attention of nuns, nurses and the entire hospital staff. When it became evident that his cancer was incurable, he asked to return to his homeland. After prolonged and tearful good-byes he was flown to Washington, on to Peshawar, and smuggled into his village in Afghanistan to die with his family.

During the major's long hospital course, my colleagues, particularly Drs. John Coughlin, John Hunt, and Karman Weatherby, provided extensive consultation and treatments without any thought of payment.

St. John's Hospital provided free care and medicines including expensive chemotherapy for over a year, and no one ever asked for any compensation.

Those who claim American doctors and hospitals are greedy should have witnessed the compassion and love provided to Major Gulabbidin by the staff of St. John's Hospital and my physician friends.

Working tirelessly behind the scenes, the most effective booster of the Afghan effort in the United States was Hasan Nouri. I first met Hasan at the fundraiser in Sacramento and was immediately impressed by this trim, athletic, immaculately dressed intellectual.

A Georgia Tech trained engineer, Hasan spent more time working for the Afghan cause than in his own career. He traveled repeatedly to Washington, to Peshawar, and inside Afghanistan, bringing information and providing all manner of assistance. Almost single-handedly he ensured the Afghan rebels would not be forgotten.

In January 1981, President Ronald Reagan said, "Those who say we live in a time when there are no heroes just don't know where to look."

We need to look no further than my friend, Mr. Hasan Nouri, to find one of the most influential heroes of the Afghan Resistance.

When I returned to the US in 1985 I feared the *mujahideen* would be slaughtered or have to leave their country, for I knew they would never surrender. I also believed their hopes of defeating the Soviet hordes were futile.

I was wrong. When the Afghans began to receive substantial military supplies, particularly after the arrival of Stinger ground-to-air missiles, the Soviets suffered defeat after defeat. The economic drain of the war became increasingly problematic in the USSR.

In early 1989, to the amazement of the entire non-communist world, the Afghans triumphed and the Russian Bear slunk back to his lair. The Berlin Wall came down, Soviet communism as a world threat crumbled, and the Cold War drew to a close. The Afghans had endured. The Afghans had prevailed. The Afghans had won. The entire world reaped the benefits of their success.

After the withdrawal of USSR forces, most observers predicted the *mujahideen* would sweep into Kabul, quickly overwhelm the communist Afghans and wreak their vengeance in a terrible blood bath. But this was not to be. Rival ethnic and tribal groups, now heavily armed, began to turn their guns on each other.

The central government could not be stabilized, and all aid from pro-western countries ceased. First one Afghan political party or ethnic group would seize power, then be defeated by another group which was soon ousted by another. Progressive destruction of the cities resulted from the constant civil war. Kabul, damaged very little during the Soviet occupation, was now devastated by the fighting, and refugees who had streamed from Pakistan into the capital were forced into the countryside. Many were lost in the minefields of their homeland.

Ostensibly because of continued fighting, the United States withdrew all support. Whether this was truly the reason for such loss of interest, or if a deal had been struck with the Soviets during the Geneva negotiations was not known.

General Mohammed Yousaf, head of the Afghan Bureau of Pakistan's Inter-Service Intelligence, stated in his book, *The Bear Trap:*

"To me, the evidence, albeit circumstantial, points to a covert decision by their main backer—the United States—that the mujahideen should not be allowed an outright military victory. I believe they could have had their triumph despite their quarrels if it had been in the United States' interest. Unfortunately, it was not."

There are many who believe a deal was made in Geneva between the U.S. and the Soviet Union. The Soviets would withdraw all their troops from Afghanistan, if the US would cease all support to the *mujahideen*.

The battling between political factions, ethnic groups and rival tribes continued almost without let-up until April of 1992 when armed *mujahideen* entered the capital, ousted the communist regime, imprisoned President

Najibullah in the United Nations headquarters building and imposed a shaky truce. Armed men roamed the streets of Kabul waiting for a spark to ignite another conflagration. Commander Ahmad Shah Massoud was installed as Secretary of Defense and attempts were made to stabilize the central government.

In late April of 1992, Hasan Nouri called to brief me on recent developments in Afghanistan and mentioned he was going there to see if any of his relatives had survived the bitter fighting. I had missed out on my chance to enter Kabul riding on a tank with Massoud as he had promised seven years before, so I jumped at the chance to go with Hasan.

In mid-May I landed in Kabul with Hasan, Robin Pierson, a charming journalist from California who had accompanied Hasan during the battle for Khost, and Charles Fawcett, an American film producer. Earlier in the war Charley had sponsored a documentary about Afghanistan and had supported the Afghan cause from his home in London.

Young teenagers laden with Kalashnikovs patrolled the streets firing their weapons in celebration. Tanks driven by equally young troops held drag races in downtown Kabul. The night sky was streaked with rockets, tracer bullets, and heavy artillery. No leader was in power and the poorly equipped hospitals were packed with patients wounded in the fighting or those injured by fall-out from the celebrations. It was *very* unsafe for foreigners in the capital, but fortunately we had obtained the protection of Commander Abdul Haq, one of Hasan's many Afghan friends. This robust, impressive gentleman was one of the heroes of the Afghan resistance. He had been wounded several times, including the loss of one foot, and was most appreciative of the large emergency medical kit I brought for his physician. Abdul Haq spoke excellent English. He, Hasan and I enjoyed a detailed discussion of the past war and his plans for the future, then he arranged bodyguards for us and the use of a small Toyota pickup.

Several tense encounters with patrolling troops were defused by Hasan, and we were able to visit my old friend, Mr. Gailani, in his Kabul home. He seemed exhausted from all the negotiations and spoke very little. His son, however, excoriated us at length about the United States' abandonment of the mujahideen. I couldn't argue with him. He was right.

We left Kabul for Jalalabad over a tortuous cratered road littered with detritus of the long war. The highway itself was passable, but the shoulders of the road and the countryside on either side of the route were seeded with mines. Wrecked tanks and personnel carriers had been shoved aside just enough to allow trucks to use the road. Live ammunition was scattered everywhere. "Comfort stops" were confined to the road.

We met scores of large trucks groaning with supplies for Kabul, tattered refugees desperately clinging to the sides and top of each truck. In a few destroyed villages ragged occupants were eking out an existence raising poppies, waiting to see what new disaster would befall them. Vacant-eyed children wandered streets and roads, homeless and hungry but too proud to beg.

As Doris Lessing has so sagely written, *"A war ends, you bury the dead, you look after the cripples—but everywhere among ordinary people is an army whose wounds don't show: the numbed, or the brutalized, or those who can never, not really, believe in the innocence of life, of living; or those who will forever be slowed by grief."*

We met with Abdul Haq's brother, the local governor in Jalalabad, who welcomed the prospect of our establishing in his province some type of refuge for orphans of the war. At that time Jalalabad was relatively safe, enjoying the protection of Abdul Haq's troops. We returned to Kabul somewhat encouraged and, after a wonderful reunion with Hasan's relatives, prepared to leave.

Since the day of our arrival, I'd made repeated attempts to meet with my friend, Ahmad Shah Massoud, and had brought gifts for him, including pictures of us together in 1985. His office was located on an upper floor of a large building in downtown Kabul, surrounded by iron gates, a high wall and guards dripping with armament and hostility. On the day prior to our departure Hasan's diplomatic skills were successful, and an appointment with Massoud was obtained.

As we waited to be ushered into his office Massoud was summoned to an emergency meeting, and I had to be content with being received by his second in command. I left my message, the pictures and gifts with this cordial gentleman and departed, somehow knowing I'd never see Massoud again.

The visit had occurred during a small window in the organized fighting. Our plane had barely lifted off before all-out war between the various factions resumed in the streets of Kabul. On the journey home our small group vowed to concentrate its energy to help the children of Afghanistan in any way possible. Largely through the efforts of Hasan, we formed International Orphan Care. This small organization primarily funded from the pockets of board members and helpful friends, supported a small operation in Jalalabad.

In this tiny school, attempts were made to train young people in some marketable skills so they might survive. Despite repeated trips to Washington, Hasan and I were never able to obtain any financial support from our government, and this situation is essentially unchanged. With no help from the United States government, Afghan refugees remain unwelcome in the surrounding countries and are unable to survive in their homeland. Afghanistan is ripped apart by continued warfare, and subsists largely by exporting heroin and importing terrorists who find refuge there.

There are many who have said the Soviet defeat in Afghanistan was largely due to the shaky economy of the USSR, the benevolence of Mr. Gorbachev and the innate defects of Communism as a way of life. However, I choose to believe, as General Yousaf said, "No matter how many political reasons may have been espoused for the Soviet's retreat from Afghanistan, they would never have gone without the efforts of these Soldiers of God."

Against all odds the lone Afghan fighter, filled with contempt for his foes, with unflagging allegiance to his God, his tribe, his family and his land, remained undefeated.

The black pennants flutter in countless graveyards throughout the country, but Afghanistan remains unconquered. By their refusal to surrender, the *mujahideen* brought about a world in which bomb shelters were no longer necessary, the evil empire had collapsed, and people all over the globe breathed a little easier as the threat of nuclear clashes between super powers diminished. The world profited, but Afghanistan paid a terrible price.

It is the unfortunate legacy of the courageous Afghans that their role in bringing global peace was never fully realized and is already forgotten.

Over ten years have passed since my adventure. I still often awake before dawn and listen for the mullah's call. Then I think of Afghanistan and its heroic people. Perhaps this story will help others to know and remember them, establishing forever their rightful place in the recent history of our world.

# POSTSCRIPT

After the Soviet Army pulled out of Afghanistan in 1989, support from the United States to that devastated country virtually ceased. The Americans missed an unparalleled opportunity to supply humanitarian aid, clear the minefields, rebuild the shattered infrastructure and return the refugees to their homeland. The ghastly consequences of this abandonment would be far worse than any pundit could have predicted.

For over three years, various tribes and ethnic groups battled for control of the Afghan government and reduced Kabul to rubble. Smuggling and heroin production became for many the only means of survival and others welcomed terrorists into their midst and assisted in the establishment of their training camps.

While tribal warfare eviscerated Afghanistan, thousands of young men in the refugee camps of Pakistan were being indoctrinated by their mullahs into a radical perversion of Islam. These religious students were molded into an increasingly powerful movement known as the Taliban.

Fanatically devoted to their religious beliefs and extremely well supplied with sophisticated weapons of war, primarily by Pakistan, the Taliban forces moved swiftly from the south and west to conquer the unstable alliance of tribes in the north.

In 1996 Kabul fell, and soon ninety percent of Afghanistan was smothered under the oppressive edicts of the Taliban. Initially they had been welcomed by the population for ending the destructive tribal warfare; however, their radical form of Islam and its harsh practices soon alienated the people. Ahmad Shah Massoud and his soldiers withdrew into the safety of the Panjshir Valley. Guerrilla warfare ensued as in the 1980's with Massoud controlling the valley, and the Taliban controlling virtually the remainder of the country.

Terrorists streamed in, heroin poured out, and Afghanistan was relegated to occasional paragraphs on the back pages of newspapers.

As the twentieth century ended, bombing of United States military barracks in Saudi Arabia, the US embassy in Kenya and a US warship harbored in Yemen were all traced to terrorists trained in Afghanistan. The mastermind of these attacks was believed to be Osami bin Laden, scion of a wealthy family living in Saudi Arabia, whose headquarters was hidden in southeastern Afghanistan. Several cruise missiles were launched by US warships towards bin Laden's hideout with little effect. Public interest in these tragic bombings waned. Afghanistan and Osami bin Laden returned to the back pages.

September, 2001 changed everything.

On September 9, Ahmad Shah Massoud was assassinated. North African terrorists posing as cameramen exploded their camera-bomb and the Lion of the Panjshir, legendary hero of his people and my friend was no more. Two days later, commercial airliners loaded with innocent passengers were hijacked and crashed into the Twin Towers of New York, the Pentagon in Washington, D.C. and the Pennsylvania countryside. Over three thousand lives were snuffed out in the single most horrific event in United States history.

President George W. Bush promptly declared war on terrorism wherever it existed. The initial targets were Osami bin Laden, his supporters, and the Taliban in Afghanistan. Bombs and missiles rained from aircraft and ships. Afghan warriors from the Northern Alliance of tribes with a smattering of highly-trained US ground troops pressed forward. In a matter of weeks the Taliban Army was driven from Kabul and the northern mountains to their refuge in the southeastern city of Kandahar.

Shortly thereafter, Kandahar fell to the relentless pounding from US planes followed by air and ground assaults of US and Afghan forces. Osama bin Laden and the remnants of the Taliban Army were pursued into their mountain cave hideouts in the Tora Bora region near the Pakistan border.

At the time of this writing in late December, 2001, a unified government has been established in Kabul, UN peacekeeping soldiers have arrived, and humanitarian aid is pouring into the country. At long last, it seems as though peace and prosperity for Afghanistan is not only possible, but probable. However, Osami bin Laden remains at large, and the battle against world-wide terrorism is far from over.

Through all the years, Hasan Nouri's labors in Afghanistan's behalf have never diminished. Now he, I, and several others are working to re-establish our orphanage-training school in Kabul and Jalalabad. My prayer is that someday soon I will return to Afghanistan and see its people rise from the ashes of war to assume their rightful place in the history of our world—and its future.

Inshallah.